The Catholic Church

Femme fatale

Bruce Benson

Heart Wish Books

The Catholic Church: Femme fatale

Published by Heart Wish Books
Cambridge, Massachusetts

heartwishbooks@gmail.com

All Scripture quotations are the
author's paraphrase unless marked

Scripture quotations marked KJV are from
the King James Version in the public domain

Excerpts from the English translation of the
Catechism of the Catholic Church for use in the
United States of America Copyright © 1994,
United States Catholic Conference, Inc.
-- Libreria Editrice Vaticana. Used with Permission

Excerpts from the papal bull *Ineffabilis Deus,*
are from *Ineffabilis Deus*, 1854, by Pope Pius IX,
in the public domain

Library of Congress Control Number: 2022917736

ISBN: 978-0-9998039-7-4

Nonfiction – Religion – Blasphemy – Heresy – Apostasy

Nonfiction – Religion – Christian Church – General

Other books by Bruce Benson

AHA moments from the Bible

Jehovah's Witnesses Hate Jehovah

The Bible on Abortion: The shedding of innocent blood

Gay-affirming theology: An explicit exposé

Bible Talk: 50 literal drawings explained

Try my Bible Quiz

Speaking in tongues: Shamana bo-ho roe-toe

Joseph Reflects Jesus: Lifegivers

Otros libros del autor en español

La Iglesia Católica: mujer fatal

Momentos AJÁ de la Biblia

Los Testigos de Jehová odian a Jehová

La Biblia sobre el Aborto: El derramamiento de sangre inocente

Teología de la validación gay: Una exposición explícita

Charla sobre la Biblia: 50 dibujos literales explicados

¡Prueba mi cuestionario bíblico!

Hablar en lenguas: Shamana bo-jo ro-to

José refleja a Jesús: Dadores de vida

Contents

Glossary

auth — authority

believer — someone who gives their life to Jesus Christ

Cat — a member of the Catholic Church

Catch — the Catholic Church

glori — glorification

hell — the place where your soul goes to die – if you were too proud to ask Jesus to save you

homsx — homosexuality

ID — Ineffabilis Deus, by Pope Pius IX

justi — justification

KJV — the King James Version of the Bible

NT — the New Testament

OT — the Old Testament

sacs — sacraments, Catch's sacs

salv — salvation

sancti — sanctification

Scripture —the Word of God, the Holy Bible

trads — traditions

Introduction

The Catholic Church claims they have the way to Heaven.

I'll prove to you that the Catholic Church is a wrong turn, a siren luring sailors to their death, a femme fatale. I'll do that by focusing on three things: how the Catholic Church treats –

- the Bible
- salvation
- and Mary, the mother of Jesus

And in the process, I'll show you the right way to Heaven.

They publish their teachings in a book called the Catechism of the Catholic Church. It has numbered paragraphs. So, if I quote paragraph twenty-five, I'll call it CCC 25.

Bruce Benson

Chapter one

Who's the Umpire?

Before we can do an investigation of the Catholic Church, we have to set the ground rules. But whose rules do we go by? A woman who calls herself a Christian is telling people that God blesses their homsx.* She said the Holy Spirit led her to do that. Who are we to judge? She says God's Holy Spirit led her. Shouldn't we take her word for it? No. We have to know if she's right.

We do that by going to the Umpire – the Authority who makes the call. That's the Word of God, the Bible, our Rule Book. And the Bible says homsx* is a deadly sin, Leviticus 20:13. So, we know she's wrong. God's Holy Spirit is not leading her. She's acting on her own. That woman is an example of what happens when people don't respect the authority of the Bible. Okay, got it. But what does that have to do with Catch? They say they respect the authority of the Bible.

Yes, In CCC 86, Catch says the leadership of Catch, "" ... is not superior to the Word of God, but is its servant ... "" But the question is, what does Catch mean when they say – the Word of God?

In CCC 97, Catch says, ""Sacred Tradition and Sacred Scripture make up a single sacred deposit of the Word of God ... "" Oh, so, Catch has two authorities. They have their tradition, and the Bible.

Can you have two authorities?
If you're playing Scrabble and your opponent puts something on the board that isn't a word, can you do something about it? Yes, you can challenge the word. Okay, but they say it's a word and you say it isn't. Game over? No. The Scrabble game comes with a book of words. If the word is in the Scrabble book, they can play it. If it's not in the book, then they have to remove it from the board, and lose that turn.

Your opponent objects. They say yes, they do accept the auth* of the Scrabble book. But, they claim that the makers of the Scrabble game have made them an auth too. Therefore, the words they create are just as good as the words in the Scrabble book.

* See the glossary on page 7.

What has your opponent done?
They said they accept the auth of the Scrabble book. But in reality
they've cancelled the auth of the Scrabble book, and made themself the
sole auth. They can put any combination of letters on the board and say
it's a word. Now, you're not playing Scrabble anymore. You're playing
Insanity. And, it's impossible for you to win.

The Bible is the Scrabble book for Christians
The apostle Paul went to the city of Berea. He taught that Jesus had to
suffer and die – and then rise from death. The Bereans cared about the
truth. So, after they listened to what Paul said, they went to the Bible.
They did an exhaustive investigation, day after day. They asked the
Authority to make the call, and show them if what Paul said is true.

Acts 17:1-3,10-12

Catch says they accept the authority of the Bible. But, they claim that
the Maker of the Bible made them an auth too. So, the teachings they
create are just as good as what's in the Bible (and Catch decides all ties).

What has Catch done?
They said they accept the authority of the Bible. But, in reality, they've
cancelled the auth of the Bible and made themself the sole auth. Catch
puts teachings on the board that are not found in the Bible, that teach
the opposite of the Bible – and Catch calls their teachings God's Word.

You can't have two authorities any more than you can have two Gods.
Catch made themself God. Cats can't challenge them. Cats can't search
the Bible like the Bereans did to see if what Catch says is true. Cats
have to choose Catch over the Bible.

It's impossible for Cats to win.

Chapter two

Does the Bible say sola Scriptura?

There's another way to say the Bible is the only Authority. You can say
sola Scriptura. It's Latin. It means Scripture alone.

I saw a Cat priest teaching on TV. I think he was of the Cheshirite order.
A Cheshire Cat. He grinned as he declared to his flock that you can't
find the words sola Scriptura in the Bible.

He's right. You can't. You can't find the words Jesus is God either.
There's no need for the Bible to say sola Scriptura, or Jesus is God, or a
fetus is a person. Those truths are the very fabric of the Bible.

God commanded sola Scriptura –

> Do not add to, or take away from
> the things I tell you to do.
> > God, Deuteronomy 12:32

How does God feel about people adding their words to His?

> If someone claims
> to be speaking for Me,
> and in their arrogance they say things
> that I never told them to say,
> do you know what will happen to them?
> They will die.
> > God, Deuteronomy 18:20

Jesus condemns people who attack sola Scriptura –

> You enforce your traditions
> because you want to do away with
> the authority of the Word of God.
> > Jesus, Matthew 15:6

Chapter three

Whose traditions do you go by?

Explain this –

- Paul told Christians to hold on tight to traditions

- Jesus condemned those who hold on to traditions

Contradiction? No.

- Paul commanded Christians to hold on to God's traditions

- The traditions Jesus condemned are people's traditions

Next one –

- Paul said the Word of God is both Scripture and traditions

- Catch said the Word of God is both Scripture and traditions

Contradiction? Yes. Why? Because –

- The Word of God is both <u>God's</u> Scripture and <u>God's</u> traditions

Isn't that what Catch said? No.

When Catch says the Word of God is both Scripture and traditions, they don't mean God's Scripture and God's traditions. They mean God's Scripture and <u>Catch's</u> traditions.

Chapter four

What are traditions?

Traditions are teachings. They're spoken or written.

The apostle Paul wrote this to the Christians in Thessalonica –

> Hold on tight to the traditions
> that I've taught you – both those that
> I've spoken, and those that I've written.
> 2 Thessalonians 2:15

Paul told us where his traditions came from –

> I delivered to you what I
> received from the Lord Jesus.
> 1 Corinthians 11:23

Paul told us what his traditions were –

> When you received the Word of God
> that you heard from us, you received it
> not as the word of people,
> but as it truly is – the Word of God.
> 1 Thessalonians 2:13

Paul said the traditions he spoke were the Word of God. But Catch says the Pope speaks the Word of God like Paul did.

No. Paul could. The Pope can't. I'll tell you why, but first we have to ask a question in the next chapter.

Chapter five

What is the Church?

You need to know that when Catch refers to, "the Church," they mean their denomination, the Catholic Church.

In CCC 816, Catch says, ""The sole Church of Christ [is that] which our Savior, after his Resurrection, entrusted to Peter's pastoral care ... This Church, constituted and organized as a society in the present world, subsists in (*subsistit in*) the Catholic Church, which is governed by the successor of Peter and by the bishops in communion with him ... ""

Catch goes on in CCC 816 to say, "" ... The Second Vatican Council's *Decree on Ecumenism* explains: "For it is through Christ's Catholic Church alone, which is the universal help toward salvation, that the fullness of the means of salvation can be obtained ... """

In CCC 846, Catch says, " ... Basing itself on Scripture and Tradition, the Council teaches that the Church, a pilgrim now on earth, is necessary for salvation: ... Hence they could not be saved who, knowing that the Catholic Church was founded as necessary by God through Christ, would refuse either to enter it or to remain in it."

Paul warned Christians about those who create denominations. He told us to spy them out, and – mark and avoid them, because they set traps to catch the unsuspecting. They seduce people by speaking pleasant words in reverential tones.   Romans 16:17-18

Here's what the Bible says the Church is –

> Believe in the Lord Jesus Christ,
> and you will be saved.
> Acts 16:31

That's it. Believe in the Lord Jesus Christ and you're part of the Christian Church. You don't need to go to a denomination or a local church to join Jesus. It's between you and Him.

Chapter six

Why could Paul speak God's Word but the Pope can't?

Why could Paul speak the Word of God, but the Pope can't?

Because Paul was an apostle. The Pope isn't.

But in CCC 882, Catch refers to the Pope as " ... Peter's successor ... "
Catch is saying the Pope is an apostle, like Peter and Paul were.

Okay, the Pope says he's an apostle. Shouldn't we take his word for it?
Who are we to judge? No. Jesus loves it when Christians investigate
fake apostles and expose them as liars.

> You examined those who
> say they're apostles, but aren't,
> and you found them to be liars.
> Jesus, Revelation 2:2

When I say Paul spoke the Word of God, I'm not talking about teaching
the Bible. All genuine Christians speak teachings from the Bible (Paul
did too). But Paul spoke the infallible (100% trustworthy) Word of God,
that he received from God – before it was in the Bible.

But CCC 890 says, " ... Christ endowed the Church's shepherds with the
charism of infallibilty in matters of faith and morals ... "

And in CCC 891, Catch says the Pope, "" ... enjoys this infallibility in
virtue of his office, when, as supreme pastor and teacher of all the
faithful ... he proclaims by a definitive act a doctrine pertaining to faith
or morals ... "" Catch is saying the Pope is Peter's successor, and he can
proclaim traditions that are the infallible Word of God, just like Peter
and Paul did. But Catch is wrong.

I know the Pope's traditions are not from God. How? Because the
Pope's traditions are not in the Bible. Ephesians 2:20 says God used
apostles and prophets to build the foundation of the Church. That
foundation is the New Testament. We know the traditions spoken by
Peter and Paul were the infallible Word of God because their traditions
eventually became books of the New Testament. There's Romans,
Galatians, Philippians, 1 Peter, 2 Peter, and others.

Jude 1:3 says the foundation was – once delivered (KJV). That means it was built once. All of the NT was written two-thousand years ago. God told us everything He wants us to know. It's in the Bible. God no longer needs men to speak His Word the way the apostles did.

Who made the Pope an apostle?
Catch says the Pope became an apostle because of what Catch calls apostolic succession. In CCC 77 Catch says, "" ... the apostles left bishops as their successors. They gave them 'their own position of teaching authority.'" Indeed, "the apostolic preaching, which is expressed in a special way in the inspired books, was to be preserved in a continuous line of succession until the end of time.""'"

In CCC 862, Catch says, "" ... the office which the Lord confided to Peter alone, as first of the apostles, destined to be transmitted to his successors, is a permanent one ... ""

Catch says the Pope was made an apostle by other apostles. But to be an apostle you had to be personally chosen by Jesus. Only fourteen men met that qualification. They were the original twelve apostles, plus Matthias (who replaced Judas), and lastly, Paul.

Jesus created the office of apostle. In Luke 6:12-13, we're told that Jesus went to a mountain and prayed all night. In the morning He called His disciples to Him and chose twelve. He made them apostles. And on the night before He was crucified, Jesus said to them –

I chose you.
Jesus, John 15:16

What about Matthias?
When the apostle Judas Iscariot died, Matthias was chosen to replace him. But Jesus had already gone back to Heaven. So, how could Jesus have personally chosen Matthias? Wasn't he chosen by the remaining eleven apostles? And isn't that apostolic succession?   Acts 1:15-26

No. At that time, Jesus still wanted there to be twelve apostles.

But years later, Jesus did not replace the apostle James (the brother of the apostle John), when James was killed by king Herod Agrippa I. That's because the office of apostle was coming to an end.   Acts 12:1-2

Who chose Matthias?
The apostles nominated two men as candidates to replace Judas. Then they prayed to Jesus. They said –

> You Lord, are the One who knows everyone's heart.
> Show us which of these two men You have chosen.
> Acts 1:24

Jesus made His choice from Heaven. Jesus personally chose Matthias. This is also more proof that Jesus is God. The apostles prayed to Jesus. Only God is to be prayed to.

Jesus personally chose Paul too
In Acts 9:15, Jesus said He chose Paul. In Acts 9:3-6, Jesus made a special appearance from Heaven to make Paul an apostle. Paul said his apostleship did not come from men or through men. He said he was made an apostle by Jesus Christ.   Galatians 1:1

Jesus personally chose all the apostles who've ever lived. All fourteen. But Catch says men made the Pope an apostle. That rules out the Pope. You can't receive the office of apostle from a man. Jesus never gave a man the power to make someone an apostle.

What else is required to be an apostle?
When a replacement was needed for Judas, the apostles said there were certain qualifications that the replacement must meet to be an apostle. For one, they had to have been a disciple during the entire ministry of Jesus, from the day Jesus was baptized, until He went back to Heaven. But Paul wasn't one of the disciples who walked with Jesus during His ministry. Paul hated Christianity then (when his name was Saul).
Acts 1:21-22; 7:58; 8:1; 9:4,13-14; 22:4-5; 26:9-11

The twelve apostles (and others) were students of Jesus when He was here on earth. But Jesus did something special for Paul.

In Galatians 1:10-12, Paul said Jesus taught him by a direct, person-to-person revelation (from Heaven). Paul met that qualification.

Did Paul see Jesus?
Acts 1:22 says another qualification to be an apostle was that you had to have seen Jesus after He rose from the dead. In 1 Corinthians 15:3-8, Paul said that after Jesus resurrected and appeared to everyone else, He appeared lastly to him. Paul met that qualification too.

How did people know the real apostles from the fakes?
The devil was the first fake apostle. And there's been an apostolic succession of fake apostles ever since. God had to make a way for people to know which men were speaking His Word and which ones were liars.   Genesis 3:1-15; 2 Corinthians 11:13-15

Hebrews 2:3-4 says God worked supernatural miracles through His apostles. The miracles spoke for them. They separated the real from the fake. Paul said the miracles that God worked through him proved he was an apostle. Paul called them the signs of an apostle.
                    Acts 19:11-12; 20:7-12; 28:1-9

> You saw the signs of an apostle
> that God did through me.
> 2 Corinthians 12:12

Catch says the Pope is a successor to the apostle Peter. Let's see how the Pope compares to Peter. There was a disciple of Jesus, named Tabitha, who lived in a city called Joppa. She was beloved by the people. But she fell sick and died. So, the disciples sent two men to find the apostle Peter and bring him to her. God worked through Peter to raise Tabitha back to life. The news of that miracle spread everywhere in Joppa.
                    Acts 9:36-42

If God was working miracles through the Pope, it would be the biggest story in two-thousand years. There would be around-the-clock news coverage as the Pope raised the dead. But that's impossible. The miracles ended after serving their purpose of identifying the apostles. The office of apostle ended after the fourteen apostles died.

Catch says the Pope's traditions are God's Word. But that's impossible. The Pope is not an apostle. The Pope is no Peter. The Pope doesn't speak the infallible Word of God like Peter and Paul did. The Pope's words are not God's words. They're the Pope's words. The Pope is adding his own words to God's Word.

In Mark 7:13, Jesus told the Pharisees that by adding their traditions to the Bible, they were taking away the Bible's power to save people.

Suppose you invite someone to dinner. But before you sit down to eat, you sweep the floor. Then you use a dustpan and brush to sweep up the pile of dirt you've collected. Your guest expects you to put the dirt in a trash can. But instead, you pour it into a pitcher of milk.

Then you pour a glass of milk from the pitcher and offer it to your guest. They say – no thanks. And you say – but it's milk, it's good, it has vitamins. They still won't drink it. You ask them why, and they say it's because you poured dirt in it. And you say – but the vitamins are still there. And they say – no, you ruined the vitamins in the milk when you poured the dirt in it.

The Pope ruins the vitamins in the Bible by pouring in his traditions.

The real Peter said – just drink the pure milk of God's Word.

1 Peter 2:2

In Acts 20:29-31, the apostle Paul said that after he dies, oppressive wolves will infiltrate the flock and eat the sheep. He was warning his fellow Christians about a fake apostolic succession.

Whenever a group says their founder or leader is a prophet or apostle, you can be sure they have false teachings. Those denominations add to the Bible, they diminish Jesus, and they say you have to earn your salvation by doing what they tell you to do.

Chapter seven

Are you saved by faith alone or by faith plus works?

Are you saved by faith alone or by faith plus works?

The question doesn't sound right. That's because it's just an expression. It's shorthand. You're not saved by your faith <u>or</u> your works. You don't save yourself. Jesus saves you. What we really mean is – do you <u>receive</u> salvation by faith alone or by faith plus works?

The Bible says faith alone –

> Salvation doesn't come from you.
> It's an act of kindness done by God.
> God gives you salvation as a gift.
> You contribute nothing to it.
> That way you can't brag that
> you had something to do with it.
> The only thing you bring to it is your faith.
> Your faith is what you use to receive
> God's gift of salvation.
>   Ephesians 2:8-9

Now we have our Guide.

What does Catch say?
In CCC 183, Catch says, "Faith is necessary for salvation ... " And Catch says in CCC 162 that, "Faith is an entirely free gift that God makes to man ... " It sounds like Catch is saying God gives salvation as a free gift. But with men's religions there's always a catch. I'll tell you what it is, but first we need to define some words.

We just saw both Ephesians 2:8-9 and CCC 183 use the word salvation. But they could have said – justification. The word salvation can mean the complete set of stages in salvation. Or it can mean the justi stage (or the glori stage). The stages of salvation include justification, sanctification, glorification, and others.   Romans 8:29-30

We need to look at justi first. It's the heart of this argument. I want to make this easy for you. So, when the KJV calls justi – salvation, or redemption, or righteousness – I'll change it to justification, or justi.

What's justification?

Justification is a ticket to Heaven. Our Guide told us God gives that ticket as a gift. The way Paul explained it in Romans 3:24 is that believers are justified freely. The word – freely, was translated from the Greek word – dorean (the New Testament was written in Greek).

What does dorean mean?

In John 15:25, Jesus said people hated Him without a cause. It means He did nothing to deserve their hatred. The words – without a cause, are one word in the original Greek. It's our word – dorean. So, believers did nothing to deserve our ticket to Heaven. Our ticket is dorean, free.

We also need to know the word – impute. God said something in Genesis 15:6, that He really wants us to pay attention to. That's why it's quoted three times in the NT –

> Abraham believed God,
> and God imputed it to
> him as justification.
> Romans 4:3; Galatians 3:6; James 2:23

The KJV says God imputed it to him as – righteousness. It's the same thing as justi. Both words come from the Greek word – dikaios.

What does imputed mean?

Paul wrote a small book in the NT called Philemon. It's a letter to a man named Philemon about a man named Onesimus. Paul cared about Onesimus like a father cares about his son, and he was concerned because Onesimus owed Philemon some money.

So, Paul said to Philemon – put Onesimus' debt on my account. The words – **on my account**, are translated from the Greek word – **ellogeo**. When Paul wrote that Abraham's faith was imputed to him as justi, the word – **imputed**, is the Greek word – **logizomai**. Ellogeo and logizomai are cinnamons (they mean the same thing).   Philemon 1:18

Onesimus didn't pay back the money he owed Philemon. His **freedom** from debt was **imputed** to him because Paul paid his debt for him.

Every one of us owe God a debt that we've incurred because of our sin. We can't go to Heaven until we've paid that debt. But it's impossible for us to pay it. Jesus loves us. So, He paid our debt by dying on a cross. And if you truly believe in what Jesus did, then He will **impute** your **freedom** to you. You'll go to Heaven because Jesus paid for your ticket.

What's Catch's catch?
I pointed out that in CCC 183 and CCC 162, Catch said faith is necessary for justi, and that faith is an entirely free gift that God gives. <u>And</u> in CCC <u>2010</u>, Catch says justi is by God's grace, that God initiates justi, and no one can merit God's grace of forgiveness and justi. What's the problem? Catch said the same thing in CCC 2010 that our Guide said in Ephesians 2:8-9. Our Guide will approve of CCC 2010. Right?

No. You have to look under every rock. There could be poisonous snakes hiding under them. The Jehovah's Witnesses say Jesus is the Son of God. If you stopped there, you'd think they teach the same thing as the Bible. But keep digging, and you find out they teach that Jesus was created by God, and that Jesus is the archangel Michael.

The Jehovah's Witnesses' Son of God is 0% God. That's not what the Bible teaches. When the Bible says Jesus is the Son of God, it means Jesus is 100% God. The Jehovah's Witnesses' Jesus can't justify anybody.

I only told you the parts of CCC <u>2010</u> that sound right. Now I'll show you the whole story. In CCC 2010, Catch says, "Since the initiative belongs to God in the order of grace, *no one can merit the initial grace* of forgiveness and justification, at the beginning of conversion ... "

Catch says no one can merit the **initial** grace of forgiveness and **justification.** The words I've highlighted change everything. Catch says God only gives Cats an <u>initial</u> justi (and Cats have to complete it themselves). There's the catch.

And, as if that's not bad enough, Catch goes on in CCC 2010, to say, " ... Moved by the Holy Spirit and by charity, *we can then merit* for ourselves and for others the graces needed for ... the attainment of eternal life ... " It turns out that Catch's justi is not a free gift after all.

Chapter eight

Who pays for a gift?

Has anyone ever given you a gift, and told you they bought it on layaway, but they only paid the first installment, and you have to pay the rest of the installments yourself? Of course not. No one does that.

But Catch says God did that. In CCC 1129, Catch says, "The Church affirms that for believers the sacraments of the New Covenant are *necessary for salvation* ... " Catch says Cats have to pay off God's gift of justi with a lifetime of installments (and Catch collects the payments). Catch calls the payments – sacraments.

In CCC 1113, Catch says, "... There are seven sacraments in the Church: Baptism, Confirmation or Chrismation, Eucharist, Penance, Anointing of the sick, Holy Orders, and Matrimony ... "

What makes Christianity unique?
In Ephesians 2:8-9, our Guide said God gives justi as a free gift. In the verses just before that, Ephesians 2:4-7, our Guide told us why God does that. It's because He has a soft heart for us. God overflows with tender mercy. And He wants to show us how much He loves us by giving us a gift, the best gift ever, as a complete surprise – not because we gave Him something (we didn't), but because He loves us.

What gift did God give us? He gave His Son. God sent His only Son to die for us. Jesus died in our place, to make a way for us to be delivered from sin, death, and the devil – and to be spared from God's holy anger (the wrath of the Lamb, Jesus) – and to be saved from the eternal death of hell – and to give us eternal life in Heaven instead. That's justi. God paid for our gift of justi with His Son's life. <u>That's</u> why He can give us justi as a free gift.

Hebrews 2:14-15;
Revelation 6:15-17

Christianity stands alone because our God did something unheard-of. Our God took on a human body like ours – with flesh, bones, and blood – so He could be executed for our crimes. Jesus let Roman soldiers torture Him and crucify Him. God went through that to take the punishment for our sins – and to show us how serious our sin is. Our God's love for us is the most extraordinary thing that distinguishes Him as the only God. Our God is love.   1 John 4:8-10,16

The gift of God is eternal life
through Jesus Christ our Lord.
Romans 6:23 KJV

You might have noticed that I switch back and forth. I'll say – God, and then I'll say – Jesus. When Jesus was in a human body, God was in two places at the same time. God and Jesus are the same person. Jesus has always been God, and He always will be. There's only one God. And there's only one Savior – the Lord Jesus.

When the Bible says God gave His only Son to die for believers, God is teaching us by using the image of a father who sends his only son to war, and his son dies. The father gave his son to fight and die to save people from tyranny, and to preserve freedom. And God said – I'm going to do that to save you from the tyranny of sin. I'm sending **My** Son to die for **you**.

Give thanks to God.
His Gift is so awesome.
Words can't fully describe it.
2 Corinthians 9:15

If a father sent his son to war and his son died in battle, would you tell him his son didn't do enough? Of course not. But Catch tells God that the death of His Son wasn't enough.

Catch tell Cats that God gave them an incomplete justi, and they have to be co-saviors, and complete their justi themselves.

But God said –

Besides Me, there is no savior.
God, Isaiah 43:11

Sin is the problem
We sin when we break God's law. And the wages of sin is death.

1 John 3:4; Romans 6:23 KJV

Jesus lived His life for one reason – to die so we can live.

> Jesus Christ came to this
> world to save sinners.
> 1 Timothy 1:15

You're not qualified to pay for your justi
God said the sacrifice for our sins had to be sinless. Only Jesus could earn our justi because He's the only one who has no sin. Everyone else sins. Someone who sins can't pay for justi.   Exodus 12:5; John 1:29;
1 Corinthians 5:7; 1 Peter 1:18-19

Christians still sin (every day) even after we're justified.   1 John 1:8

Our justi is priceless. Only the priceless blood of Jesus could pay for it. But Catch says Jesus didn't suffer enough. And Catch tells Cats that their performance of Catch's sacs is as valuable as God's blood.

> Jesus bought eternal
> justification for believers.
> He paid for it with His own blood.
> Hebrews 9:12

The priests in the OT had to sacrifice animals every day because of sin. But in Hebrews 10:5, Jesus said to the Father – You don't want animal sacrifices. You get no pleasure from them. I'm here to do Your will. You put Me in a human body so I could be the perfect sacrifice for sin.
Hebrews 7:27

> Now, <u>once</u>, in the end of the ages,
> Jesus has appeared to put away sin.
> He did that by sacrificing Himself.
> Hebrews 9:26

The word – once, in that verse, means the sacrifice of Jesus was once for all time, never to be repeated. Justi is finished. It's perfect, completed. There are no more sacrifices. There's nothing more to do. There's nothing to complete.

Just before Jesus died on the cross, He said –

It is completed.
Jesus, John 19:30

Hebrews 7:25 says if people come to God through Jesus, then Jesus is able to justify them – <u>to the uttermost</u>. That's one word in the original Greek – panteles. It means – completely, entirely. It means Jesus is able to justify you completely – from the moment He justifies you. And it means Jesus keeps you justified forever, and ever, with no end.

One time, Jesus was dining at the house of a Pharisee. There was a woman who was a sinner, who heard Jesus was in the house. She went there and stood behind Jesus. Tears ran down her face as she wept and wailed loudly. Her tears fell on the feet of Jesus. Then she used her hair to dry His feet. And she kissed His feet.   Luke 7:36-50

Jesus told the people at the dinner that the woman was doing that because her sins were forgiven. Then Jesus said to the woman –

Go in peace, your faith has justified you.
Jesus, Luke 7:50

Jesus couldn't very well say – I've given you an initial justi. Now you need to go to Catch. They're the only ones I've authorized. You'll need to complete your justi by spending the rest of your life doing whatever they tell you to do to. Oh, and one last thing – go in peace.

What? Go in peace? How in the world could she have peace after that?

No. Jesus doesn't treat people that way. Jesus doesn't tease us with justi. He wants us to have justi. The only way He could tell her to go in peace is if He'd given her a completed justi. And He did.

Jesus assured the woman. He said – you can go on with your life now with peace of mind, because you received justi with your faith alone. You're completely justified. You know you're going to Heaven.

Isaiah 53:11 was written six-hundred years before Jesus would be crucified. It says that when God sees the sacrificial death of Jesus on a cross for the sin of the world, then God's justice will be completely satisfied. But Catch isn't satisfied. Catch want Cats to do Catch's sacs to add to the sacrifice of Jesus.

Christians don't do sacrifices. Jesus made the one sacrifice for our sins. All of our sins are forgiven – past, present, and future. We don't do a sacrifice when we sin. We confess our sin.   1 John 1:9

This is serious. It makes the difference between whether you go to Heaven or not. Once you do Catch's sacs you've rejected Jesus, you're lost. God won't accept your sacrifice for sin. He only accepts the sacrifice that Jesus made for sin.

Cats need to decide. Catch or Christ. You can't have both.

Cats think they possess something they can use to complete their justi. But to God it's an abomination (it makes Him sick). Your sacs are no good. Your sacs are a stench in God's nose. They're the road to hell. Justi's not for sale.

> Your efforts to justify yourself
> are like filthy rags to Me.
> God, Isaiah 64:6

This verse teaches the simplicity of justi –

> If you say that Jesus is your Lord,
> and you believe in your heart that
> God raised Jesus from the dead,
> then you will be justified.
> Romans 10:9

Jesus told stories to teach us who He gives justi to, and who He doesn't. In Luke 15:11-32, Jesus told a story about a man who had two sons. The **younger** son took his father's money and spent it on wild parties.

But when he was in his right mind, he went to his father and said – I've done you wrong, and I've sinned against God (that's called repentance, an essential element in genuine faith).   Acts 2:37

His father was overjoyed. He hugged his son and kept kissing him. His father didn't send him to jail. And he didn't make him pay back the money. The son didn't have to do any works, or do any sacs.

Instead, his father clothed him in the best garment, and put the family ring on his finger. His father called everyone and said – my son came home! Let's have a party! And everyone was happy. Well, not everyone. The **older** son was angry. He told his father – hey! I've been killing myself working for you all these years. And I've never done anything wrong. Where's **my** party?

The **older** son is all those who think they deserve justi. They present their own efforts to God and think He will reward them by giving them justi. <u>Cats</u> are the **older** son. Jesus told that story to rebuke Cats who think they can complete their justi with Catch's sacs. No. You can't make God owe you justi.The **older** son wants justi because of what <u>he</u> did. The **younger** son received justi because of what <u>his father</u> did.

The **younger** son is those who receive justi as an **<u>UNDESERVED</u>** gift.

Jesus told another story in Luke 18:9-14. Two men were in church, praying. <u>One</u> of them was checking off all the things he does for God. He even patted himself on the back for doing more than God required. The <u>other</u> man was so ashamed of himself that he kept his head down. He said – God, it's me, the sinner. Please have mercy on me. Jesus said <u>that</u> man went home justified, but the bragging man didn't.

Did you hear what Jesus said? He said that man – <u>went home</u> justified. Jesus didn't say – okay, that's a good start – that man got his initial justi. So, after he does a lifetime of sacs for Catch, I might accept him as fully justified. No. Jesus said that man went home completely justified. That man asked God to give him justi. The other man delighted himself by listing all the things he was doing to complete his justi.

God withholds justi from people who don't appreciate how valuable it is. Who don't appreciate the price Jesus paid for it. God only justifies people who realize they can only receive justi as a gift, because they have nothing of any worth to pay for it. Psalm 34:18

God gives justi to people who are brokenhearted and crushed because of their sin. People who mourn over their sin. Humble people. People who hate themselves. They know they're helpless, hopeless sinners.

If Ted Bundy receives justi by faith alone, then when God looks at Ted Bundy, He will see the holiness of Jesus. If Mother Teresa does not receive justi by faith alone, it won't matter how many good deeds she does, or how many of Catch's sacs she does. Ted Bundy will be in Heaven forever but Mother Teresa will never see Heaven.

> When you try to justify yourself
> by external rituals, you're saying
> you have no use for Christ.
> Galatians 5:4

Cats say – no, Paul's talking about the law of Moses there – we're not completing our justi by obeying the law of Moses, we're completing it by doing Catch's sacs. No, Cats. Works can't make you deserve justi. Not the law of Moses, or Catch's sacs, or any other works. You're trying to add to the perfect sacrifice of Jesus.

There's only two states you can be in. You're either 100% justified, or you're 0% justified. There's no in-between. There's no such thing as Catch's initial justi that needs to be completed. Trying to complete your justi by doing sacs isn't Christianity. It's what the people of the religions of the world are trying to do.

All you need is Jesus –

> When Jesus was in a human body,
> everything there is to God was in that body.
> Jesus is 100% God. Jesus is complete.
> Colossians 2:9

When you have Jesus, you're complete.
Colossians 2:10

You'll spend the rest of your life trying to pay for Catch's justi. But Justi's not a mortgage you pay off. There's no scoreboard.

God gives you justi when you truly believe. Your acceptance is guaranteed, regardless of prior conditions. You can't be turned down for any reason. And your rates can never go up.

God said He will give you justi as a free gift, and He meant it. God is honest. He has integrity. He's not a liar. God doesn't play cruel games. There's no tricks, no surprises, no hidden charges.

How many times does God have to tell you justi is free?

Let me put it another way –

God's justi is free, free, free, free, free, free, free, free, free, free, free, freeeeeeeeeeeeeeeeeeeeeeeeeeeeeeeeeeee!!!!!!!!!!!!!!!

Fuhree already.

Chapter nine

Who does God justify?

Suppose someone you love was about to be killed. And you're the only one who can save them. Would you? Yes? But, what if the only way you could save them was to lose your life?   John 15:13

Okay, now there's another person who's about to be killed. This is someone who hurt you. They stole from you. And they wanted to make you look bad, so they said you did evil things. But you didn't do them. You're the only one who can save them. But to save their life, you have to give up **your** life. Would you die to save someone who made themself your enemy? God did.

Romans 5:8-10 says Jesus gave His life to save our lives – when we were making ourselves His enemies.

Romans 4:5 says God justifies – the **ungodly**.

God doesn't say – go work on yourself, clean up your act, do some sacs, and come back when you're good enough, and then I'll justify you. No. God gives you complete justi when you're a filthy sinner. And guess what – filthy sinners are the only kind of people God justifies (the ones who know what they are, and admit it).

> I'm not here to justify the righteous.
> I'm here to justify sinners.
> Jesus, Matthew 9:13

That's sarcasm. Jesus is taunting the amateur do-it-yourselfers. Those who reject His ready-made justi, and make their own justi from a kit. The ones who justify themselves. The so-called righteous.

Introduction to chapters ten and eleven

The idea that you have to complete your justi, is something you won't find in the Bible. But Catch says there are Bible verses that agree with them. In the next two chapters we'll look at some of those verses.

There's Philippians 2:12, where the apostle Paul tells Christians to work out our salvation. And James 2:24, where James says we're justified by works, and not by faith alone.

When you come to verses like those two, that appear to say you have to complete your justi yourself, or that you're justified by works and not by faith alone, the first thing you need to do is look to our Guide to keep you on the right path.

Why do I say we have our Guide? Because without our Guide, the Bible seems contradictory and confusing. We have to establish the absolute truth. Then we can study the Bible with confidence.

If you've obeyed God and received His free gift of justi, then God will send His Guide to walk with you. So, study the Bible diligently. Look up words in the original languages. Read commentaries about the verse you're studying. Keep searching, keep digging – keep thinking about the verse day and night. Ask God to tell you what the verse means. God will answer your prayer. Then you'll know the truth.

> Ask, and it will be given to you.
> Seek, and you will find.
> Knock, and it will be opened to you.
> Jesus, Matthew 7:7

> If you lack wisdom, then ask God for it.
> God wants with all His heart to give wisdom
> to those who put their trust in Him.
> James 1:5-7

> God rewards those who won't let anyone
> or anything stop them from studying the Bible.
> Hebrews 11:6

Chapter ten

Did Paul tell Christians to complete our justification?

The apostle Paul wrote this to Christians –

> Work out your salvation.
> Philippians 2:12

The words – work out, were transated from one word in the original Greek. It's – katergazomai. It means – to finish, to bring to completion. Is Paul agreeing with Catch that we need to complete our justi? No.

Remember, in the Bible, the word salvation can mean one of the stages of salv – such as justi, sancti, or glori (and keep in mind also, that when Catch say there's stages to salvation – they mean there's stages to justi).

In Romans 13:11, Paul wrote – our salvation is nearer now than when we first believed. He's talking about the glori stage.

So, in Philippians 2:12, when Paul tells us to complete our salv, which stage of salv is he talking about? Our Guide is here, and He said it's not justi. It's not glori either. We can't give ourselves eternal, sinless bodies. And we can't predestinate or foreknow ourselves. That leaves sancti.
> Romans 8:29-30; 1 Corinthians 15:53

But we can't complete our sancti either. Only God can. Yes, and that's one of the wonderful paradoxes of Christianity. Jesus completes our sancti, and He commands us to complete our sancti. Jesus tells His followers to do things that are impossible for us to do, like this –

> Be perfect, like God is perfect.
> Jesus, Matthew 5:48

Okay, then what about justi? No, God never tells people to complete their justi. On the contrary, He condemns those who try that.

What's the difference between justification and sanctification?
Justification is instantaneous. Jesus was at the house of a man named Zacchaeus. And when Zacchaeus showed that he had genuine faith, Jesus said – today, justi happened in this house.   Luke 19:1-10

But, justi doesn't change us. Justi just **says** we're something we're not. Justi calls us 100% sin<u>less</u> when we're 100% sin<u>ful</u>. Justi says we're like Christ when we're not like Christ.

And while justi <u>is</u> a ticket to Heaven – it's <u>not</u> a license to sin. So, that's why, after God justifies us, He begins the sancti stage. Sanctification is the gradual process that makes us like Christ. It's when God washes away our sin from the inside out. Sanctification is incremental.

In 1 Thessalonians 4:3, Paul wrote that what God wants for Christians is our sancti. The word sancti is # 38 in the Greek dictionary, in the back of the Strong's Concordance. It means holiness. Obeying God's law is holiness. God wants Christians to become free from sin, like Jesus.

On the night before Jesus was crucified, He met with His twelve apostles. It's known as the Last Supper. You can read about it in the Gospel of John, chapters 13-17. During those last hours together, Jesus did something startling. He washed the apostle's feet. One reason why Jesus did that was to teach us the difference between justi and sancti.

Jesus said to Peter –

> Peter, you walked around
> and got your feet dirty.
> But you don't need to take a bath.
> You just took one.
> You don't need to take another bath.
> Someone who's taken a bath
> is already clean.
> You just need to wash your feet.
> Jesus, John 13:10

Jesus used taking a bath and washing your feet as an illustration.

The bath represents your justi, and washing your feet represents your sancti. Jesus is making the point that once you're justified, you don't need to be justified again. But you do need the daily washing of sancti because your feet get dirty from walking around in this sinful world.

Sancti is the lifelong work you do to become what God said you are.

Justi cost you nothing. But it cost Jesus everything. Becoming like Jesus costs you everything.

> You can't become My disciple
> if you're not willing
> to be killed for My cause.
> Jesus, Luke 14:27

God does our justi. But sancti is different. God does our sancti. And we do our sancti –

> I am the Lord. I sanctify you.
> God, Leviticus 20:8

> Sanctify yourselves.
> God, Leviticus 20:7

√ God cleanses believers. He purges us of filth. God snips and prunes us like trees. He lops off bad branches. He cuts away whatever is sinful and worthless, so we can bear more fruit.   John 15:2

• God commands believers ourselves to strip off every unnecessary thing that weighs us down, and to deflect the sins that come at us from every direction, so we can run our race with steady determination.
                                                                Hebrews 12:1

√ God loves believers. So, He puts us through strict training. It's compared to punishment and **scourging**. The word "**scourgeth**" in Hebrews 12:6 (KJV), is the same Greek word used in John 19:1 for the flogging done to Jesus by the Roman soldiers. God puts us through painful experiences for our good. He lets us suffer so we'll mature. His training humbles us, and reveals our sinfulness to us.   Hebrews 12:5-14

• The apostle Paul orders believers to train ourselves like he does. Paul takes himself prisoner. And he beats his own face black and blue. He fights his sin like a boxer with brass knuckles. 1 Corinthians 9:26-27

Christians declare war on our alcoholism, porn addiction, bitterness, discontentment, refusal to forgive people, greed, lust, covetousness, racism, sinful anger, pot smoking, pride, etc., etc., etc.

Do we do that by flicking a switch? No. Sancti doesn't just happen. We have to do painful, hard work – over our whole life. It's a long, difficult journey. We go through spiritual rehab. Old addictions and bad habits must die. We stop wasting God's precious gift of time. We can't live like we did before. Now we must obey.

We do that by following Jesus. We obey Jesus because He is our Lord. He showed us what to do. He lived an active life. Jesus isn't lazy. He gave His all. And Jesus commands His followers to live like He did.

> Follow Me.
> Jesus, Luke 9:23

> We who've received Christ
> are to live our lives His way.
> Colossians 2:6

> Walk in His footprints.
> 1 Peter 2:21

In Romans 12:1-2, God commands Christians to renew our mind. We do that by being immersed in Bible study.

> Everything in the Bible was
> breathed into it by God.
> It's a treasure chest of learning,
> disciplining, and training in
> righteousness, to make a child
> of God complete, and fully equipped
> to do all kinds of good works.
> 2 Timothy 3:16-17

My personal experience is that my sancti is something I need to work on every waking hour (and sometimes when I'm asleep and dreaming).

When I'm with people, if we're not talking about the Bible, then I start gossiping, lying, talking too much about useless things, engaging in idle chatter, and enjoying vulgar things. I need to make an all-out effort, no let-up, with constant vigilance, praying often.

I spend hours a day studying the Bible at my desk. When I'm out walking, I listen to Bible teachers on Mp3s. I need to keep learning more and more about God from the Bible. I <u>need</u> to, and <u>love</u> to, keep my mind on the Bible – seeking, thinking, thirsting, and asking.

Becoming holy is what makes you a Christian. It's what makes you different. Jesus is returning to earth. Do you want to be doing your favorite secret sin when Jesus returns? No. When Jesus returns He wants to find you busily engaged in the work He gave you to do.

No, Cats. Paul didn't tell Christians to complete our justi. He told us to give everything we have to our sancti.

Chapter eleven

Did James say we're jusified by our works?

James wrote this –

> You're justified by works,
> not by faith alone.
> James 2:24

Why would James say that? In Ephesians 2:8-9, Paul said – we're justified by faith, and <u>not</u> by works (our Guide). Are Paul and James confused? Contradicting each other? No. Paul and James are in perfect harmony. Really? Yes. God is the Author of the Bible. All the books of the Bible are of one mind. We can see that by looking at what Paul and James said about Abraham.

√ Paul said it was impossible for Abraham to be justified by works.

Romans 4:1-8

• James said Abraham was justified by works.   James 2:21

What? I know, that <u>sounds like</u> a contradiction. But I needed to show you that, so we can get to this –

√ When Paul said it was **impossible** for Abraham to be justified by works, Paul quoted Genesis 15:6 –

> God gave Abraham justification
> because Abraham believed what God said.
> Romans 4:3

• And when James said Abraham **was** justified by works, James also quoted Genesis 15:6 –

> God gave Abraham justification
> because Abraham believed what God said.
> James 2:23

So, Paul and James taught the same thing – there's only one way to be justified. God only gives justi to those who don't rely on their works, and receive justi by faith in the sacrificial death of Jesus Christ.

But the question remains – why, in James 2:24, did James say you're justified by works, and not by faith alone? Well, we know James isn't going against our Guide. So, James must have said what he said, the way he said it, in order to make a point. We have to find that point.

To do that, we have to back up to the question James asked ten verses earlier, in James 2:14. James asked – what good is it if someone says they have faith, but they don't have works – can faith save them?

That sounds like the same thing as when James said you're justified by works, and not by faith alone.

Yes, it does. But, in the next two verses, James explained his question by putting it another way. He said – suppose some fellow Christians don't have warm clothing, and they barely have enough to eat. And you say to them – go in peace, be warm, be full. But you don't give them any food or clothing. What good is that?   James 2:15-16

Then, James said – in the same way, if your faith in God doesn't produce works, then your faith is <u>dead</u>, because it's <u>alone</u>.   James 2:17

Oh, so, by – faith alone, James means faith that's alone because it doesn't <u>do</u> anything. And back in verse 14, when James said – what good is it if someone says they have faith? – he meant – what good is it if people **just say** they have faith – but they never <u>act</u> on it? And when he said – can faith save them? he meant – can <u>that</u> kind of faith save them? (your words only mean something if you act on them)

But, in James 2:21, James said Abraham was justified by works. Yes, and then he said –

> Abraham's works teamed up
> with his faith, and his works
> made his faith complete.
> James 2:22

Oh, so it was Abraham's faith that was made complete by his works.

Next, James quotes Genesis 15:6 to make sure we know he's in 100% agreement with our Guide. –

> God gave Abraham justification
> because Abraham believed
> what God said.
> James 2:23

And then we come to our verse. Cats think this is <u>the</u> Bible verse that will support their justi-in-stages teaching –

> You're justified by works,
> not by faith alone.
> James 2:24

But, Cats are wrong. James 2:24 is the conclusion of the answer to the question in James 2:14. The question that can be asked this way – what good is it if someone says they have faith, but they don't want to do works – will God give justi to someone who has that kind of faith?

James said you're justified by works and not by faith alone – because a faith that's alone (because it has no intention of doing spiritual works for God) is not the kind of faith that God will give justi to (because, as we know, God **gives** us justi, we don't justify ourselves).

John 2:23 says there were many people who believed in Jesus. But the next verse says Jesus didn't believe in <u>them</u>. Jesus knows everyone and everything. He knew they didn't have the genuine faith – the faith that wants to **<u>OBEY</u>** God.

But why did James say it the way he did? Why did he say – you're justified by works and not by faith alone? James learned that from his Teacher, Jesus, the Great Wordsmith. Jesus spoke tight-fitting, finely honed sentences. Jesus didn't waste words. He could boil down a teaching into the fewest words. Doesn't that confuse people? Yes! To most people, the sayings of Jesus are indecipherable riddles. Jesus designed them that way to conceal the truth from them – because **they** closed their eyes and ears to the truth.

But, His sayings are windows to the truth – to those of us who want the truth. We understand Jesus perfectly.   Matthew 7:6; 13:10-17

Jesus told a woman – your faith justified you. James said Abraham was justified by works. Those statements are puzzling. But both Jesus and James know that those of us who love the truth will look to our Guide. We know we're justified by Jesus and not by our works. We won't deliberately misinterpret their words to try and make them agree with the traditions of men.   Luke 7:50; James 2:21

Both the woman and Abraham received justi with their faith. They both had the kind of faith that God rewards with justi. They had the faith that will produce holy works, and never stop producing them. They're not like the ones in Luke 8:13, who began the work, but then fled.

And guess what. James is in complete agreement with our Guide (Who said in Ephesians 2:8-9 that we can't receive justi by our works but only by our faith). In the next verse, Ephesians 2:10, our Guide said God justifies us – to good works. God doesn't justify us because of our good works. He justifies us so we can do good works. We do works because of what God worked into us. James is waking people up – do works!

Jesus said – it's those who endure to the end who will be justified. He didn't mean we become justified by enduring. He meant that by enduring, we prove our faith is genuine, we prove we are justified. It all hinges on one thing – do Christians do works to complete our justi, or do we do works because God gave us a completed justi? Catch says we do works to complete our justi. God said we do works because He gave us a completed justi. God is right.   Matthew 10:22

Christians do works to glorify God, to honor Him, to worship Him. God gets all the credit, and all the glory. We do works because God is great, because God is amazing. He takes sinners and turns us into Christians who do holy works. It proves that God can do anything.

> When you bear much fruit, you show that you are
> My disciples, and My Father is glorified.
> Jesus, John 15:8

Chapter twelve

Who do Catholics worship?

What's the worst thing that could happen when men add their traditions to the Bible? It's this – they turn the mother of Jesus into a goddess, and they worship her.

Cats protest when we accuse them of worshiping Mary. But they're like the child who says they didn't eat the cake, when they're covered from head to toe in chocolate.

As part of their worship of Mary, Cats engage in repetitive chanting of a prayer called the Ave Maria, or – the Hail Mary. The words to it are found in CCC 2676 and 2677 –

> " ... *Hail Mary [or Rejoice, Mary]:*
> *Full of grace, the Lord is with thee:*
> *Blessed art thou among women*
> *and blessed is the fruit*
> *of thy womb, Jesus.*
> *Holy Mary, Mother of God:*
> *Pray for us sinners, now and*
> *at the hour of our death: ...* "

Cats made up part of their prayer by taking words from Luke 1:26-38. That's when God sent the angel Gabriel to tell Mary something. Catch calls it the Annunciation (announcing).

In Luke 1:28, Gabriel greeted Mary with these words –

> Hail, highly favored.
> The Lord is with you.
> You are blessed among women.
> Luke 1:28

Did Gabriel say anything to make us think Mary is worthy of worship?

• Gabriel said – hail. It was just a greeting. After Jesus rose from the dead, He met two of His female disciples on the road. Jesus said – hail. He meant – be happy. Matthew 28:9

• Gabriel told Mary she's – highly favored (Catch says – full of grace). The words – highly favored, are just one word in the original Greek. It's # 5487 – charitoo. It appears only one other time in the NT.

It's in Ephesians 1:6, where Paul told Christians that God – **made us accepted**. That's two words in the Greek. There's # 2248 – us. And then there's our word, # 5487, charitoo, which is – **made accepted** (when Paul said God made us accepted, he meant God justified us).

The verses <u>before</u> Ephesians 1:6 are about God's grace. Paul said God justifies us so that His glorious grace will be praised by all creation. The word charitoo means grace – God's grace. When God justifies us, He graces us. God makes us accepted – by His charitoo, His grace, His great love for us – for the praise of <u>His</u> glory, and no one else's.

Then Paul goes on to say in verse 7 that our sins are forgiven by the riches of God's grace – because Jesus shed His blood for us. Paul keeps talking about God's grace. It's all about <u>God's</u> grace.

From their misuse of the word charitoo, Catch created a monster. Cats attribute something to Mary that belongs only to God. The reason Catch translates charitoo as – full of grace, is because Catch teaches that **Mary** is a dispenser of justifying grace.

That's not what Gabriel meant when he said – hail, highly favored. What he meant is that Mary was blessed because she'd been chosen by God to be the mother of the Savior, Jesus (as he explained to her in Luke 1:31-38). Mary is a recipient of grace. She's not a giver of grace.

• Gabriel told Mary that the Lord was with her. The Angel of the Lord said the same thing to Gideon. We don't worship Gideon. Judges 6:12

• Gabriel told Mary she was – blessed among women. Jael was said to be – blessed <u>above</u> women. We don't worship Jael.   Judges 5:24

We compared Scripture with Scripture. Now, we've learned the truth. Gabriel didn't say anything to make us think Mary is to be worshiped. The Bible overrules Catch's traditions.

I'll show you what Cats are doing – from their own words. It will shock you. It angers all of us who fight to defend God's honor.

Who is their All-Holy One?

Cats say things in their prayer that Gabriel didn't say, that no one in the Bible ever said. They call Mary – holy Mary. Cats pray, "Holy Mary, Mother of God, pray for us sinners." They call her Holy Mary because they think she never sinned (unlike "us sinners").

In CCC 2677, Catch calls Mary, " ... the All-Holy One.... "

There's no way Catch can spin that to make it okay. That title belongs only to God Himself. In the OT, God is called the Holy One – no less than forty times. By calling Mary the All-Holy One, Catch is trying to give more honor and glory to Mary than the Bible gives to God.

> I am the Holy One.
> God, Hosea 11:9

Mary's not the All-Holy One. The Bible says God is –

> You alone are holy.
> Revelation 15:4

There are four "living ones" around God's throne. All day, and all night, they say –

> Holy, holy, holy,
> Lord God Almighty.
> Revelation 4:8

Jesus is called the Holy One in Mark 1:24, Luke 1:35, Acts 3:14, and in Acts 2:27 (quoted from Psalm 16:10).

Catch is doing a wicked thing when they call Mary the All-Holy One.

Who is their sinless one?

In CCC 493, Catch says, "The Fathers of the Eastern tradition call the Mother of God "the All-Holy" (*Panagia*) and celebrate her as "free from any stain of sin.... "" (Catch calls Mary – "the Mother of God")

In 1854, Pope Pius IX wrote an official teaching called – Ineffabilis Deus (that's Latin. It means God's greatness can't be expressed in words). Catch refers to it in CCC 411, and they quote it directly in CCC 491.

Remember, Catch says the Popes are apostles. And, Catch says the Popes can deliver new teachings from God, like the apostles Peter and Paul did. And Catch tells Cats that they must accept the new teachings that come from the Popes – as if those teachings are coming from God.

Pope Pius IX wrote that Mary is, "... ever absolutely free of all stain of sin, all fair and perfect .... "

Pope Pius IX wrote, "The Catholic Church, directed by the Holy Spirit of God, is the pillar and base of truth and has ever held as divinely revealed and as contained in the deposit of heavenly revelation this doctrine concerning the original innocence of the august virgin .... "

The Pope used the words of 1 Timothy 3:15, where Paul said the Church built on Christ is – the pillar and base of truth. Christ is the Word of God, and in the Bible, the Word of God says everyone who passes through this world is stained with sin.   Romans 5:12

The defenders of Catch's trads object. They say I'm taking that verse too literally. They say if I claim that Mary had sin because everyone has sin, then I'm saying Jesus had sin, because "everyone" would include Jesus.

Here's the thing, Cats.

If you're going to try and use Bible verses to defend your tradition, then the rest of the Bible has to support your tradition. It doesn't. The Bible cleary states over and over that Jesus is sinless. But it never, ever gives any hint of a reason to make us think Mary was sinless.

Jesus was part of "everyone" because He was fully human (He was fully God too). Jesus knew exactly what we go through with all of our temptations to sin, because He was in a human body just like ours. Jesus did something though, that no one else can do. He never sinned.

Hebrews 4:15

In CCC 411, Catch says Mary "... committed no sin of any kind during her whole earthly life." Catch is describing Mary with the words the Bible uses to describe Jesus.

Jesus committed no sin.
1 Peter 2:22

The Bible says this about Mary, and everyone (except Jesus) –

If we say we have no sin,
we deceive ourselves, and
the truth is not in us.
1 John 1:8 KJV

Mary would shriek in horror if she heard what Catch is saying about her. If Mary never sinned, then she didn't need Jesus to save her. But Mary confessed that she was a sinner when she said –

I rejoice in God my Savior.
Luke 1:47

The Angel of the Lord told Mary's husband, Joseph, to call the Son Mary gives birth to – Jesus, because He will save His people from their sins. And Mary called Jesus her Savior – because she too needed to be saved from her sins. Romans 3:23 says everyone has sin. That's why the Holy One is the only one who could justify us, and give us eternal life.

Matthew 1:21

God gave Him who does no sin,
to be the sacrifice for our sins.
2 Corinthians 5:21

Whose conception do they honor?
In CCC 508, Catch says this about Mary, "**....** from the first instant of her conception, she was totally preserved from the stain of original sin and she remained pure from all personal sin throughout her life."

In his ID, Pope Pius IX wrote, "**...** the conception of Mary is to be venerated as something extraordinary, wonderful, eminently holy, and different from the conception of all other human beings .... "

You could delete the words – Mary, her, and she, from those two quotes and replace them with – Jesus, His, and He – because they perfectly describe the conception and life of Jesus. Catch stole the conception and life of Jesus, and gave them to Mary (she doesn't want them).

In Luke 1:31, Gabriel told Mary that Jesus will be conceived in her womb. In verse 34, Mary asked him how this could be, seeing she's never had physical relations with a man. Gabriel said Jesus will be conceived – <u>without a human father</u>. It was Jesus – and Jesus alone, who was miraculously conceived.

In CCC 722, Catch says Mary was, "... conceived without sin .... "

No. Jesus was conceived by Power from on High, by God's Holy Spirit. Jesus was God's Son – literally. And Jesus is God's only begotten Child. When the Bible says Jesus is the Son of God, it means Jesus <u>is</u> God. It means Jesus is holy, holy, holy. It means Jesus is sinless. It means Jesus was conceived without sin. No one else was conceived that way.
Matthew 1:20; Luke 1:35; John 3:16

It's the conception of Jesus that is to be venerated as something extraordinary, wonderful, eminently holy, and different from the conception of all other human beings – not Mary's! She was the young woman God chose to carry Jesus in her womb and give birth to Him. That's it. Nothing more. Mary was a good girl, but a sinner in need of justi, the same as everyone else.

By describing Mary in terms that belong to Jesus, Catch is showing us what they really think of Jesus.

Who is their source of holiness?
In CCC 2030, Catch says a Cat does this, "**....** From the Church he learns the *example of holiness* and recognizes its model and source in the all-holy Virgin Mary...."

The Bible never says Mary or any other person is a source of holiness. That's because God is the only source of holiness. Romans 15:16 says believers are made holy by God's Holy Spirit. Hebrews 13:12 says Jesus made believers holy with His own blood.

In John 17:17, Jesus prayed for His followers. He asked the Father to use His Word, the truth, to make His followers holy.

And Jesus said this to the apostles –

> Now you are clean, through the
> Word that I've spoken to you.
> Jesus, John 15:3

Romans 8:29 says God conforms believers to the model of Jesus. He is the Holy One. Mary is not the model of holiness.

In CCC 867, Catch says this about the Catholic Church, "**....** in Mary she is already all-holy."

Did you know Catch teaches these things? Are you shocked?

The Mary of the Bible is the humble mother of Jesus. Catch's Mary is a goddess. And their goddess is the face of Catch. Who is this goddess that gives Catch her power? Who is she, really? We'll get to that.

Who do they pray to?

In their Hail Mary prayer, Cats say, "Holy Mary, Mother of God, pray for us sinners."

Cats say that's no different than asking a fellow Christian to pray for you. No, it's not like that at all. Your fellow Christians are here on earth. You go to them, or call them on the phone. Mary's in Heaven. The only way to ask her to pray for you – is to pray <u>to her</u>.

The Bible doesn't need to say the words – don't pray to Mary. The Bible makes it clear that praying to or worshiping anyone other than God is idol worship.

> Don't put another god in My face.
> Do not make a statue of someone
> and bow down to it to worship them.
> God, Exodus 20:3-5

> Idolators, and all false ones,
> will have their place in the lake
> that burns with fire and brimstone.
> That's the second death.
> Revelation 21:8

The first death is the death of the body. The second death is the death of the soul – for people who worship a goddess as though she's God.

In CCC 2679, Catch says this about Mary, "....When we pray to her, we are adhering with her to the plan of the Father.....We can pray with and to her ...."

Believers pray to God –

> Oh, You Who hears prayer.
> To You will all Your people pray.
> Psalm 65:2

In Luke 11:1, the disciples of Jesus asked Him to teach them to pray.

Jesus told them to pray – our Father, Who is in Heaven. Jesus tells His followers to pray to the Father, not "the Mother."

The Bible never instructs anyone to pray to a person.

Talk to Me.
I give the answers.
God, Jeremiah 33:3

Who is their source of mercy?
In CCC 2677, Catch says this about Mary, "**....** we address ourselves to the "Mother of Mercy," the All-Holy One....."

To have mercy on someone means you do something for them because they're suffering, and it hurts you to see them hurting.

In 2 Corinthians 1:3, Paul wrote that God is – the <u>Father</u> of mercies. That's because God shows the greatest mercy when He forgives sinners who trust in the sacrificial death of His Son, Jesus.

Catch wants to use the Bible to back up their traditions. <u>But</u> – take your Strong's Concordance and look up the hundreds of verses that use these words when talking about <u>God</u> – compassion, compassions, consolation, grace, gracious, graciously, lovingkindness, mercies, merciful, mercy, pitieth, pitiful, pity, tender (mercies).

Where are the verses that use those words for Mary? There are <u>none</u>. The Bible never speaks of Mary as being a source of mercy, or as the one people should go to for mercy. God is the Source of Mercy.

People cried out to Jesus for mercy in Matthew 15:22, 17:15, Mark 10:47, and Luke 17:13.

> Cast all your mental distress on God,
> because He cares about you.
> 1 Peter 5:7

> Come to Me, all of you
> who toil and are burdened.
> I will give you rest.
> Jesus, Matthew 11:28

There's no Mother of Mercy in Heaven. There is only the Father of Mercy. Catch took God's title and gave it to their goddess. Catch gives to their goddess the kind of respect, the kind of awe and reverence, that is to be given only to God.

Who do they call out to in times of trouble?
In CCC 971, Catch says, "....From the most ancient times the Blessed
Virgin has been honored with the title of 'Mother of God,' to whose
protection the faithful fly in all their dangers and needs....."

There are dozens of verses in the Bible telling believers that God
protects us in all our dangers and needs. Not one verse says that about
Mary. Do you see the problem? Catch quotes the Bible as though they
accept the Bible as the Umpire. But then Catch teaches things that are
not only not found in the Bible, but are a slap in the face to God's glory.

Here are some of the verses in the OT –

> People who do what's right will
> suffer many afflictions, but the Lord
> delivers them out of all of them.
>> Psalm 34:19

> The Lord will cover you with
> His feathers, and under His
> wings you will trust.
>> Psalm 91:4

> The Lord is a strong tower.
> A righteous person runs into it
> and they are safe.
>> Proverbs 18:10

> I will love You, Oh Lord.
> You are the source of my strength.
> The Lord is my rock, and my
> fortress, and my deliverer.
> My refuge, in Whom I will trust.
>> Psalm 18:1-2

> They hid a net to catch me.
> Oh Lord, pull me out of it.
>> Psalm 31:4

Here's more from the ID of Pope Pius IX, in case you want to read it. I've broken it up into paragraphs to make it easier to read.

Pope Pius IX said this about Mary, "... in her who is the glory of the prophets and apostles, the honor of the martyrs, the crown and joy of all the saints; ... "

"... in her who is the safest refuge and the most trustworthy helper of all who are in danger; in her who, with her only-begotten Son, is the most powerful Mediatrix and Conciliatrix in the whole world; ... "

" ... in her who is the most excellent glory, ornament, and impregnable stronghold of the holy Church; in her who has detroyed all heresies and snatched the faithful people and nations from all kinds of direst calamities; in her do we hope who has delivered us from so many threatening dangers ..."

" ... Let all the children of the Catholic Church ... continue to venerate, invoke and pray to the most Blessed Virgin Mary, Mother of God, conceived without original sin ...

"... Let them fly with utter confidence to this most sweet Mother of mercy and grace in all dangers, difficulties, needs, doubts and fears ... "

"... Under her guidance, under her patronage, under her kindness and protection, nothing is to be feared; nothing is hopeless. Because, while bearing toward us a truly motherly affection and having in her care the work of our salvation, she is solicitous about the whole human race ... "

The things Pope Pius IX wrote there have nothing to do with the Mary of the Bible. None of them can be found in the Bible. They are pure fiction. That's nothing but goddess worship. Idol worship. Worshiping Mary instead of God.

The fact that Mary is the mother of Jesus, does not mean she has anything to do with the things Jesus does. Stop talking about her as though she's Jesus. Stop giving her titles that belong to God. He doesn't like that. And no, Cats, Mary is not your mom.

Here's what the Bible says –

> Deliver me, oh my God, out of the
> hand of the wicked, out of the hand
> of the unrighteous and cruel person.
> You are my hope, Oh Lord God.
> I've put my trust in You since my youth.
>> Psalm 71:4-5

> Call upon Me in the day of trouble.
> I will deliver you.
> And you will glorify Me.
>> God, Psalm 50:15

> Worship the Lord your God.
> Serve Him, and no one else.
>> Jesus, Luke 4:8

> You alone are God.
>> Psalm 86:10

Where are the verses that tell believers to call out to Mary in times of trouble? There are none.

> Cast your burden upon the Lord.
> He will put His shoulder next to yours,
> and He will be your support.
>> Psalm 55:22

> The Lord will help everyone
> who cries out to Him,
> everyone who cries out
> to Him in truth.
>> Psalm 145:18

Who do they commit their souls to at death?
In CCC 2677, Catch says this about Mary, "**....** We give ourselves over to her now, in the Today of our lives. And our trust broadens further, already at the present moment, to surrender "the hour of our death" wholly to her care.... "

Just before Jesus died on the cross, He cried out loudly, and said –

> Father, I put My soul in Your care.
> Jesus, Luke 23:46

Stephen was killed because he followed Jesus. And as Stephen was dying, he looked up and saw Jesus in Heaven. Jesus was standing, and waiting for Stephen to join Him.

And Stephen said –

> Lord Jesus, I put my soul in Your care.
> Acts 7:59

Jesus and Stephen surrendered the hour of their death wholly to God's care. Catch tells Cats to surrender their hour – wholly to Mary's care.

Once again, Catch is deleting God, and replacing Him with Mary.

Who is their intercessor?

For <u>Christians</u>, Jesus is <u>the Intercessor</u>. Jesus intervened when He died to justify us. He made peace between us and God. He settled our differences, made reconciliation.

But justified people still sin. So, Jesus is in Heaven making intercession with the Father, right now, on our behalf. Jesus talks about us with the Father. Jesus does something for believers that we can't do for ourselves – He keeps us justified.

In CCC 2674, <u>Catch</u> says, " ... Jesus, the only mediator .... "

In CCC 2634, Catch says this about Jesus, " .... He is the one intecessor with the Father on behalf of all men, especially sinners. He is "able for all time to save those who draw near to God through him, since he always lives to make intercession for them .... ""

Catch quoted the Bible in CCC 2634. They quoted Hebrews 7:25, which says Jesus is the intercessor. And they cite Bible verses at the bottom of the page. They have Romans 8:34, which says Jesus is at the right hand of God making intercession for believers. And they have **1 Timothy 2:5** (we'll look at that verse at the top of page 105).

<u>But</u> Jesus warned us about people who say one thing – and do another. They honor Jesus with empty words. Their hearts are far from Him.
Matthew 15:3,7-9; Mark 7:6-9,13

In CCC 968 and 969, Catch says this about Mary, " .... she is a mother to us in the order of grace .... "This motherhood of Mary in the order of grace continues uninterruptedly from the consent which she loyally gave at the Annunciation and which she sustained without wavering beneath the cross, until the eternal fulfilment of all the elect..... ""

In CCC 969, Catch says this about Mary, ""... Taken up to heaven she did not lay aside this saving office but by her manifold intercession continues to bring us the gifts of eternal salvation .... "" In CCC 970, Catch says, ""Mary's function as mother of men in no way obscures or diminishes this unique mediation of Christ .... ""

What? In no way obscures or diminishes the unique mediation of Christ? Are they joking? Dear Cats, you need to read CCC 968 and 969 over and over until you see what Catch is doing.

CCC 969 says Mary's alleged grace – "continues uninterruptedly." No! It's the grace of Jesus that continues uninterruptedly. The Bible says Jesus – ever liveth to make intercession for them (for believers).

Hebrews 7:25 (KJV)

When the child who's covered in chocolate finally admits they ate the cake, then they start making excuses why they <u>had</u> to eat the cake. Cats say they had to call Mary the intercessor because of 1 Timothy 2:1-3. That's where Paul <u>tells believers to make</u> prayers and – <u>intercessions,</u> for all those who are in governmental authority.

The word – intercessions, in that verse, is # 1783. It's used only one other time in the NT. That's in 1 Timothy 4:5, where the KJV translates it – prayer. It comes from # 1793, which is the word – intercessor – the word used for Jesus in Hebrews 7:25 (the verse Catch cited) which says Jesus is the Intercessor.

Does any of this mean that Mary (or anyone else) can be an Intercessor like Jesus? No, of course not. In Acts 25:24, the word # 1793 is used to say people complained about Paul.

How do we solve this once and for all? Easy. Context. In CCC 969, Catch said Mary has a "saving office," and that she, "by her manifold intercession continues to bring us the gifts of eternal salvation."

No. Those are lies. Why? Because Mary didn't die on a cross to justify believers. Jesus did. Mary is not God. Jesus is. Mary is not the Intercessor. Jesus is.

Read this, and be shocked –
In CCC 969, Catch says this about Mary, "" ... the Blessed Virgin is invoked in the Church under the titles of Advocate, Helper, Benefactress, and Mediatrix ... "" Catch gave Mary the title – Mediatrix. They twisted a title that belongs only to Jesus – and gave it to Mary.

Jesus is the Mediator. There is no Mediatrix. Hebrews 8:6; 9:15; 12:24 all say Jesus is the Mediator. And **1 Timothy 2:5** says there is one God and one Mediator between God and people – the Man Jesus Christ.

> You can't get justi from
> anyone other than Jesus.
> God did not give us anyone else
> that we must go to for justi.
> Acts 4:12

> Look to Me and be justified,
> everyone in all the earth,
> because I am God,
> and there is no other.
> God, Isaiah 45:22

CCC 969 says Catch invokes Mary under the title – Helper.

The title Helper appears one time in the NT –

> The Lord is my Helper.
> Hebrews 13:6

Only one has the title – Helper. That's the Lord. Not Mary.

CCC 969 says Catch invokes Mary under the title – Advocate.

The word advocate appears in the Bible. First John 2:1-2 says that when Christians sin, we have an advocate with the Father – Jesus Christ the righteous. And it says He is the – propitiation for our sins. It means that God's justice was satisfied when Jesus died for sinners,.

Catch's goddess is their "Advocate." But Catch's goddess didn't die for sinners. She didn't satisfy God's justice. Jesus did. Catch's goddess is not the Advocate. Jesus is. The word advocate is # 3875. It's used only for Jesus, in 1 John 2:1, and for the Holy Spirit of Jesus, in John 14:16,26; 15:26; 16:7, where it's translated – Comforter.

Catch stole that title from Jesus, and from His Holy Spirit, and gave it to their goddess.

In CCC 494, Catch has a quote that they attribute to Irenaeus, which says this about Mary, " ... "Being obedient she became the cause of salvation for herself and for the whole human race ... ""

Mary didn't do that. The words Catch used in CCC 494 about Mary are a perfect description of what Jesus did. Philippians 2:8 says Jesus became obedient by giving Himself over to death on a cross.

And the Bible says this –

> Jesus was God's Son.
> He proved that He understood
> what obedience means, by enduring
> the suffering that He went through.
> And because He obeyed God perfectly,
> Jesus became the Author of eternal salvation
> for everyone who obeys Him.
> Hebrews 5:8-9

In his ID, Pope Pius IX says this about Mary, "... All our hope do we repose in the most Blessed Virgin — in the all fair and immaculate one who has crushed the poisonous head of the most cruel serpent and brought salvation to the world ... " That's a murderous teaching.

The serpent who was in Eden, was the devil himself –

> That old serpent, called the Devil and Satan.
> Revelation 12:9 KJV

> And the devil that deceived them was
> cast into the lake of fire and brimstone.
> Revelation 20:10 KJV

It isn't Mary who crushes the serpent's head. In Genesis 3:15, God told the serpent that **Jesus** will crush his head.

It was Jesus (not Mary) who became the cause of salvation (only for believers). Jesus took away the devil's power by taking away the power of sin. How? When Jesus died and rose from death, God forgave all the sins of believers. Christians put all our hope in Jesus, not Mary.

1 Corinthians 15:55; Hebrews 2:14-15; 1 John 1:9

In CCC 829, Catch says, "" ... in the most Blessed Virgin the Church has already reached that perfection whereby she exists without spot or wrinkle ... ""

Catch says they became without spot or wrinkle – because of Mary (which would mean Mary is without spot or wrinkle). Peter wrote that believers were bought with the precious blood of Christ, who was like a Lamb – without blemish and without spot. Catch stole that too.

1 Peter 1:19

Pope Pius IX put a warning in his ID. He said, " ... Hence, if anyone shall dare — which God forbid! — to think otherwise than as has been defined by us, let him know and understand that he is condemned by his own judgment; that he has suffered shipwreck in the faith; ... "

" ... that he has separated from the unity of the Church; and that, furthermore, by his own action he incurs the penalties established by law if he should are to (sic) express in words or writing or by any other outward means the errors he thinks in his heart ... "

So, if Cats don't worship Catch's goddess – then Catch takes away their "initial justi." That's further proof that Catch's justi is not God's justi. When God justifies you – He keeps you justified. When God gives you justi, He never, ever takes it back, and you can never, ever lose His justi. It comes with a guarantee from the Manufacturer.

John 6:37,39-40; 10:27-30; 14:6; Romans 8:14-17,28-39;
Ephesians 1:13-14; Philippians 1:6; 1 Peter 1:3-5

One more thing. Once, at a wedding, Mary told Jesus that the host ran out of wine. Then she told the waiters to do whatever Jesus tells them to do. They did. And Jesus did a miracle. But no, Cats, that does not mean Mary is the Mediatrix. The Bible won't support that.   John 2:1-11

Did Mary sleep with her husband?
In CCC 499, Catch says, "The deepening of faith in the virginal
motherhood led the Church to confess Mary's real and perpetual
virginity ....And so the liturgy of the Church celebrates Mary as
Aeiparthenos, the "Ever-Virgin.""

If it were true that Mary is the Ever-Virgin (it isn't), it would prove
Catch is wrong when they say Mary never sinned (they are wrong).
Mary was married to Joseph. If she never had sex with Joseph, then she
sinned by defrauding her husband of sex.

In 1 Corinthians 7:3-5, Paul wrote that married Christian couples must
obediently and cheerfully give each other sex. He said the wife's body
belongs to the husband, and the husband's body belongs to the wife.
They must never deny each other sex. Paul said refusing to have sex
with your spouse is to – defraud them.

Now, don't go trying to accuse Paul, or God, of saying a man can rape
his wife. They're not. Violence toward a spouse is wrong. It's sin. God,
and Paul, said a husband is to love his wife like Christ loved the
Church. And Christ gave His life for the Church. The thing is, people
can only have sex with their spouse. So, God, and Paul, are making a
point. The point is that part of the agreement, the contract of marriage,
is that you're to dutifully give your spouse sex.   Ephesians 5:25

Catch's perpetual virginity of Mary is a demonic, man-made holiness.
Paul warned in 1 Timothy 4:1-5 that there are people who call
themselves Christians, who teach things that Paul called – teachings
from devils. They tell Christians they can't do things that God said they
<u>can</u> do. They forbid marriage, and they forbid meat, telling Christians
they have to be vegetarians.

Catch says Mary was always a virgin, that she never had sex with her
husband Joseph. But the Bible says this –

> Before Joseph and Mary came together,
> Mary became pregnant through the Power of the Highest.
> Matthew 1:18

It says – <u>before</u> they came together. That means they're going to come together, later. What does come together mean? It's # 4905 in the Strong's. It can mean two or more people met for any reason.

But, in 1 Corinthians 7:5, Paul used the word to mean sex – sexual relations between a married man and woman.

That verse, Matthew 1:18, is about Jesus being conceived in Mary's womb. There was no sex involved in that conception. But the concept of pregnancy and the fact that Joseph and Mary were married, is enough context to know what's meant by the words – Joseph and Mary came together. It means they had sex.

Catch said Mary never sinned. Now they claim she never had sex with her husband. Why? Because Cats would be less willing to worship a goddess who has sex. It would destroy the illusion of deity.

In CCC 971, Catch says this about Mary, "" ... The Church's devotion to the Blessed Virgin is intrinsic to Christian worship ... ""

Catch does go on to say in CCC 971, " ... This very special devotion . . . differs essentially from the adoration which is given to the incarnate Word and equally to the Father and the Holy Spirit ... "

Then, in CCC 971, Catch says, " ... The liturgical feasts dedicated to the Mother of God and Marian prayer, such as the rosary, an "epitome of the whole Gospel," express this devotion to the Virgin Mary."

Once again, Catch gave a respectful tip of the hat to God. And then it's back to their true love. Look at what they say about Mary, what they do to worship Mary – the liturgical feasts dedicated to her, Marian prayer, done – to express devotion to her.

In CCC 971, Catch said they have for Mary, a "very special devotion ."

Look closely at what Catch said in CCC 971, "" ... The Church's devotion to the Blessed Virgin is intrinsic to Christian worship ... "" That's worship. Catch worships Mary, or what they call Mary.

In CCC 966, Catch says this about Mary, "" ... when the course of her earthly life was finished, was taken up body and soul into heavenly glory, and exalted by the Lord as Queen over all things ... ""

In his ID, Pope Pius IX said this about Mary, "... she has been appointed by God to be the Queen of heaven and earth, and is exalted above all the choirs of angels and saints, and even stands at the right hand of her only-begotten Son, Jesus Christ our Lord ... " That sounds like the way the Bible talks about Jesus.

> God has highly exalted Jesus,
> and given Him a name which
> is above every name. So that in
> the name of Jesus every knee
> will bow, in Heaven, and earth,
> and under the earth. And everyone
> will say that Jesus is the Lord,
> to the glory of the Father.
>   Philippians 2:9-11

Pope Pius IX said Jesus is – Mary's "only-begotten Son." No! The Bible says Jesus is – God's only-begotten Son. The Bible never calls Jesus Mary's only-begotten Son.

> For God so loved the world,
> that He gave His only begotten Son,
> so that whoever believes in Him
> will not perish, but will have
> everlasting life.
>   John 3:16

Catch talks about Mary the way the Bible talks about God –

> Yours, O Lord, is the greatness, and the power, and the
> glory, and the victory, and the majesty, because all that
> is in Heaven and earth is Yours. Yours is the Kingdom,
> O Lord, and You are exalted as head above all.
>   1 Chronicles 29:11

Mary's not exalted. Mary's not the Queen. There is no Queen of Heaven. There's only the King. God is the King.

> The Lord is our King.
> He will save us.
>> Isaiah 33:22

> The Lord is King forever and ever.
>> Psalm 10:16

> Sing praises to our God. Sing praises.
> Sing praises to our King. Sing praises.
> He is greatly exalted.
>> Psalm 47:6,9

In Matthew 27:11 and John 18:37, Jesus said He is the King of God's people. When Jesus returns, He will have this written on His robe –

> King of kings and Lord of lords.
>> Revelation 19:16

God told us how He feels about the queen of heaven –

> The children gather wood, and the fathers kindle
> the fire, and the women knead their dough,
> to make cakes for the queen of heaven,
> and to pour out drink offerings to other gods,
> so they can provoke Me to anger.

> Do they provoke Me to anger? says the Lord.
> Do they not provoke themselves to their own confusion?

> Therefore, says the Lord God. Behold, My anger and My fury
> will be poured out upon this place, upon man, and upon beast,
> and upon the field, and upon the fruit of the ground.
> And it will burn, and not be quenched.
>> God, Jeremiah 7:18-20

In his ID, Pope Pius IX actually mentions Jesus. But then he goes on to talk about Mary in the very words that are only to be used for Jesus. He starts with this, "... We give, and we shall continue to give, the humblest and deepest thanks to Jesus Christ, our Lord ..."

Oh, how nice, he thanked Jesus. But do you know what he thanked Jesus for? For this, " ... because through his singular grace he has granted to us, unworthy though we be, to decree and offer this honor and glory and praise to his most holy Mother ... "

Unbelievable. The way Pope Pius IX talks about Mary, sounds like the worship that's given to God in Heaven –

> The four and twenty elders fall down
> before Him Who sits on the throne,
> and worship Him Who lives forever,
> and cast their crowns before the throne,
> saying, You are worthy, Oh Lord,
> to receive glory, and honor, and power.
> Revelation 4:10-11

The way Pope Pius IX talks about Mary, sounds like the worship that's given in Heaven to the Lamb, Jesus Christ –

> Worthy is the Lamb Who was slain
> to receive power, and riches, and strength,
> and honor, and glory, and blessing.
> Revelation 5:12

God said this –

> I am the Lord. That is My name.
> And I will not let My glory
> be given to a strange god.
> I will not let My praise
> be given to a statue.
> God, Isaiah 42:8

You can read Deuteronomy 13:6-11 to find out how God feels about those who entice people to worship other gods.

Catch say Mary obediently complied when she was told she would be the mother of Jesus. And Catch says therefore, Mary is a giver of salvation along with Jesus. No, Cats, the Bible won't support that. Mary had absolutely nothing to do with salvation.

The apostle Peter went to the house of a man named Cornelius. When Peter walked through the door, Cornelius fell down to worship him. But Peter said – get up, I'm a man, like you. And Mary is a woman, a person, like us. She's a humble, obedient Christian, the same as any other Christian.   Acts 10:25-26

You might say, well, sure, Catch says those things about Mary in the CCC, but you don't know what Cats are doing, maybe they don't worship Mary, maybe they just worship Jesus. No. I do know what Cats are doing. I do know the results of Catch's teachings.

I walked into a Catholic chapel in Boston. The first thing you see in the entryway is a touchscreen. Touch it, and there are three options. Two are about Mary. I selected those. There's accounts of Mary appearing to people, all over the world, over many years. Here's some of them –

In 1717, in São Paulo, Brazil, the local governor was planning to visit the city of Guaratinguetá. The people wanted to honor him with a feast. Fishermen were sent to catch some fish. But they caught nothing. So, they pleaded to Mary, and cast their net. They caught a statue of Mary.

They retrieved the statue and cast their net again, and they caught plenty of fish for the feast. They named the statue, Our Lady of the Conception.

Does that sound familiar? The disciples of Jesus spent a whole night fishing and caught nothing. In the morning, Jesus came to them and told them to cast their net. And they caught all the fish they needed.
                                              John 21:1-14

Another story takes place in Luján, Argentina. Statues of Mary were put in boxes and placed on an ox cart.

But the cart wouldn't move. So, they took the statues out of the boxes, and then the cart moved. They said Mary made it move. So, a chapel was built there. And the statue of Our Lady of Luján became a much loved image in Argentina. The story also claims that the Argentine flag's colors of blue and white are from the colors of the statue of Our Lady of Luján.

There's a story from Quebec, Canada. The faith of the people of Quebec was fading. So, the parish priest consecrated himself to Mary. He prayed every day in public, and preached about Mary to the faithful. Because of that, the people's faith began to revive. Then, in 1879, they needed to build a new church. The building materials needed to be brought over a frozen river.

But the winter of 1879 was mild, and the river didn't freeze. So, the priest told his flock to turn to Mary through prayer. And on March 16th, 1879, a cold blast froze the St. Lawrence River. The river stayed frozen for a week, long enough to bring the building materials over it.

In El Cobre, Cuba, sometime in the early 1600s, three sailors were on the water when a violent storm arose. The sailors prayed to Mary for help, and the storm calmed. Then they saw what appeared to be a girl floating in the water. It was a statue of Mary, with the inscription, "I am the Virgin of Charity." The clothes of the statue were dry, even though it had been floating in the sea.

Catch is stealing miracles from Jesus. The Bible says the disciples of Jesus were in a boat when a great storm hit. And it was Jesus who calmed the storm. Matthew 8:23-27

More stories –

In 1858, in Lourdes, France, Mary appeared as the Immaculate Conception to a thirteen-year-old girl, and asked her to pray, and to make sacrifices for sinners.

In 1489, in Bavaria, Germany, a young boy drowned. His mother placed his body at the feet of a statue of Mary, and the boy rose from death.

In 1626, the Spanish Governor-General of the Philippines sailed from Mexico with a carved wooden statue of Mary. He had a safe voyage. So, the statue was given the title, Our Lady of Peace and Good Voyage. Every time that statue was on a ship, the voyage was safe and successful.

In the 1700s, Christians in La Vang, Vietnam had to hide in the jungles because of persecution. It was very difficult finding safe water to drink. But, in 1798, Mary appeared to them. She was holding the infant Jesus. Mary told them she knew how much they were suffering. And she showed them some leaves to make a tea that would be safe to drink.

And ever since, Our Lady of La Vang has been venerated, even among some who aren't Christians. A chapel to Mary was built in the 1820s.

As I stood in the entryway of the chapel writing down these stories, a woman entered. She saw the image of a statue of Mary on the screen. She stood next to me, smiled at me, and then proceeded to touch the image of Mary over and over, in adoration.

Cats say they don't worship Mary, but the evidence says otherwise. They're being taught to cry out to Catch's goddess – instead of Jesus. Cats give their heart to the goddess, instead of to Jesus.

It's time to answer the question – who is Catch's goddess? Look at Catch's churches. There's statues of the goddess out front, sometimes even on the altar. Catch is worshiping their goddess like she's God.

So, we have to ask the question– who is it that wants to be worshiped like God? The answer is – the devil.

Before the devil became the prince of darkness, he was a bearer of light, called Lucifer. God blessed Lucifer about as much as a being can be blessed. But it went to his head. Lucifer became proud. And he nursed an evil, burning desire in his heart.

Lucifer looked up at God on His throne, and said to himself – that's
where I belong.   Isaiah 14:13-14; Ezekiel 28:11-15

Lucifer wanted to take God's place and be worshiped as though he was
God. That's when he became the devil, the enemy of God. The devil
said to Jesus – fall down and worship me. Jesus told him – it is written,
worship the Lord your God, and serve Him only.   Matthew 4:8-10;
                                                    Deuteronomy 6:13-14; 10:20

Not many people want to worship the devil. So, the devil disguises
himself by appearing to be an angel of light. That's how he tricked Eve.
But the devil will, "be brought down to hell, to the sides of the pit."
                                                    Genesis 3:1-24; Isaiah 14:15 KJV;
                                                    2 Corinthians 11:14; Revelation 20:10

The devil has used Catch over many centuries, to trick billions of
people into worshiping him through Catch's goddess.

In CCC 867, Catch calls themself, "she." Catch is the femme fatale, the
fatal lady. She's the devil in disguise.

The devil is a liar and a murderer.
Jesus, John 8:44

Catch rejects the authority of the Bible. They reject God's way of
justification. And they worship a goddess. The Catholic Church is not a
Christian church. Catholics are not Christians.

Catch says they're leading Cats to Heaven. But they're not. Catch is
leading Cats to join the devil in hell.

General index

A

B

F

G

wept and wailed with joy
because she received justi from
Jesus with her faith alone ... 52
wicked, Catch is doing
a wicked thing, by calling
Mary "the All-Holy One" ... 85
windows to the truth, the sayings
of Jesus are – to those of us
who love the truth ... 78
wisdom, ask God for it ... 63
without spot and blemish,
Jesus is. Mary wasn't ... 107
Witnesses, Jehovah ... 45
wolves who call
themselves apostles ... 39
woman saved by faith alone ... 52,78
words, empty ... 103, see 76 too
Wordsmith, Great, Jesus is ... 77
worship, idol ... 93,98
worst thing, 81

Z
Zacchaeus ... 67

Scripture index

Index of quotes from the Catechism of the Catholic Church
and the Ineffabilis Deus

Cover Image: ID 44978586 © Andreykuzmin | Dreamstime.com

ISBN10: 1-63199-203-1
ISBN13: 978-1-63199-203-2

EnerPower Press
P. O. Box 841
Gonzalez, FL 32560

energion.com
pubs@energion.com
850-525-3916

TABLE OF CONTENTS

PREFACE

Before I moved to Shanghai, many wise teachers and writers sacrificially shared with me from their experiences about life abroad. "Learn the language quickly," they insightfully advised. "Immerse yourself in the culture. Find a support group. Expect and prepare for culture shock. Be patient with others. Laugh at yourself often." A particularly excellent resource full of such advice, and one that serves as a complementary companion to my work, is Michael H. Romanowski's and Teri McCarthy's, *Teaching in a Distant Classroom: Crossing Borders for Global Transformation* (IVP Books, 2009). I remain indebted to Romanowski, McCarthy, and so many others for their advice that helped me better transition to another country. However, one needed piece of advice specifically directed toward academicians serving internationally has fallen between the cracks—practical advice about how to research while living in a new and challenging environment.

Need for this advice set in quickly for me after settling into my new routine in China. After learning where to shop, meeting my colleagues, and preparing for classes, I turned my attention toward beefing up my recently completed doctoral dissertation for publication. Step one, I thought, was easy: navigate to some relevant web pages. Step two was unexpected: find out why I can't navigate to these relevant web pages! And just like that, I was introduced to the so-called "Great Firewall of China," China's pervasive, and aggravatingly intrusive, internet censorship. Days of frustration later, I discovered ways to navigate around it. This turned out to be the first of many obstacles to my research abroad.

Sometimes I navigated these new obstacles with the grace of an Olympic diver. More times than I care to confess, however, my reactions were less than stellar. On a few occasions, I'm embarrassed to say, my dilapidated, but completely innocent, desk received unwarranted blows from this frustrated abuser. Some simple tips and tools for this Visiting Lecturer of New Testament, who simply wanted to research and write while living in a distant land, would have provided some much-needed solace. And, by extension, my

desk would have also breathed a deep sigh of relief! My desire to help other researchers in similar, challenging situations is why I write this brief book.

I can't take full credit for the advice that follows. After all, nothing in life is accomplished autonomously, including writing books. Many of my colleagues at Global Scholars (www.global-scholars.org), the organization I serve with, have lived and researched abroad much longer than I have. Their indirect contributions via conversations over the years weave through every page. Some of them provided input specifically related to this book. I deeply wish that I could mention all of these sacrificial scholars by name, but most serve (or, one day might serve) in undisclosed locations around the world. Simply mentioning their names in a book directed toward Christians could jeopardize their jobs and/or their well-being. I know who you are. More importantly, God knows who you are; and he will reward you accordingly. Thank you for your input! I can, however, publicly thank three wonderful colleagues: Katrina Korb, Senior Lecturer of Psychology and Education and Head of the Department of General and Applied Psychology at the University of Jos, Nigeria, offered wonderful insights from the perspective of someone who researches in Africa; Rhonda Campbell, my wife and Visiting Instructor of Oral English at Shanghai Normal University, gave invaluable input at various steps along the way; and Richard Alexander, Minister of Music and Children at Memorial Baptist Church in Norwood, North Carolina (U.S.A), kindly tweaked the final manuscript for me on a visit to Shanghai.

As you read the following tips and tools, you will quickly learn that I write as a Christian to other Christians. More specifically, for the task at hand, I write as an academic missionary to other academic missionaries, though the nature of my topic clearly makes it applicable across a wide range of religious and philosophical perspectives. (As an aside, I struggle at length with whether or not to use the term "missionary" since it is such a politically charged term in many locales around the world; I opted to retain it because most of my readers understand the term even if they would themselves prefer a different one and because it remains the simplest

way to reference an important aspect of what we do). Long gone are the days when authors think that they can realistically write with a detached objectivity. Even with a topic as seemingly neutral as researching abroad, I would fool no one if I try to conceal my essential motive in writing this book: to serve God's Kingdom as a believer in Jesus Christ—the resurrected messiah, redeemer of humanity, and sovereign Lord of our universe. For this reason, I dedicate this book to Jesus, who, aside from being God's perfect missionary to humanity, commands us to love the Lord with our heart, soul, *and* mind!

INTRODUCTION:
OF MISSIONARIES AND SCHOLARS

Somewhere in the long journey of your education you heard God's call to scholarship. Maybe a professor nudged you in that direction, or perhaps it was your unquenchable thirst for knowledge. And, since you're reading this brief book, somewhere along the way God called you to serve abroad. With degree in hand, you courageously left family, friends, and security in order to serve academia in a distant classroom. Years of preparation have paid off, and now you live at the intersection of two vocational loves: mission and scholarship.

As a missionary, you're called, among other things, to travel, to learn a new culture, to speak a different language, and to eat exotic food. As a scholar—a label I use for simplicity, realizing that most of us, out of justifiable humility, would likely never attach it to ourselves—you're called, among other things, to teach, mentor students, grade papers, and direct graduate students. There is, though, one additional task that any missionary-scholar particularly struggles to fulfill: research (a term that I use in this book to collectively include, and at times use interchangeably with, writing and publishing). Research is an academic itch that all scholars live to scratch. Scratching this itch, while living in your own culture, is challenging enough. Emails. Advising students. Class preparation. And the list goes on. When you move to a locale where resources are scant, electricity is infrequent, and "turning on the air conditioning" in 100 degree weather might mean "opening the window," then advancing your field becomes exhaustingly more complicated.

It is, to say the least, much easier to write and research while working from your home country in a plush, air conditioned library than in a loud, smoke-filled office which you share with five other professors. But fret not! There is hope. In most circumstances, you can fulfill that deep longing to push your discipline forward. Helping you do this is the purpose of this book—to offer tips and tools for researching and writing while serving internationally.

I briefly mentioned a couple of these tips and tools in a 2013 article in the *Journal of The Evangelical Theological Society* (*JETS*): "The American Evangelical Academy and the World: A Challenge to Practice More Globally." My basic argument there is that, in light of America's flooded academic market, more evangelical scholars should consider practicing their disciplines abroad. Given your personal sacrifices to live missionally, this argument for you is a no-brainer. What might concern you more is a subsidiary question I ask: "Can one serve abroad and advance scholarship at the same time?" I answer "yes." But, I only offered a few passing suggestions on how to do it (e.g., use of e-books and hiring assistants), suggestions that this book builds upon.

Before adding to these comments with more tips and tools, I should clarify what qualifies me to write this book and also clarify who will most benefit from it. I have lived and researched in and around Shanghai, China for four years. During that I time, I published a monograph (*Of Heroes and Villains: The Influence of the Psalmic Lament on Synoptic Characterization*, Wipf & Stock), three peer reviewed journal articles ("The American Evangelical Academy and the World," which I mentioned above, and "New Testament Lament in Current Research and Its Implications for American Evangelicals," both in *JETS*; and "China's Intelligentsia: A Strategic Missional Opportunity" forthcoming in *Evangelical Review of Theology*), several book reviews, the book you are now reading (*Researching Abroad*), and I am currently underway with a new book for the popular press. These few publications written while living in Asia are not paradigm shifting works that will forever change my fields nor do they make me the guru of researching abroad. But, while researching and writing these works, I did pick up a number of tips and tools that seem worth passing along to you. For future editions of this book, I would love to hear by email about the tips and tools you use in your specific setting: kcampbell@global-scholars.org.

Scholars who fit into the following three categories will most benefit from this book. First, I write for those who will soon—or, who have just recently—move[d] abroad but not necessarily for

those who have lived internationally for years, though seasoned academic missionaries might find a few tools to add to their own well-worn toolboxes. Since I focus on scholars who have moved from one place to another and since I frequently reference their previous home, I struggle with how to succinctly reference their previous locale. I could use the word "stateside," but some of my readers hail from Canada and beyond. "The west" sometimes proves too grammatically cumbersome, though probably all of my readers lived there. I choose, therefore, to use the word "home" in referencing your sending culture, though I am fully aware of its inadequacies; your new culture is now your home. More accurately, our home is actually nowhere in this universe; rather, our home is being prepared by Christ himself (John 14:1–4), a place where no eye has seen, no ear has heard, and no mind can understand (1 Corinthians 2:9). With this nuance in mind, please read patiently my references to your "home" culture.

Second, I focus on those serving in the world's more challenging places, where a country's general infrastructure is yet to provide stable internet, electricity, and similar amenities. Third, I direct these tips and tools to researchers who primarily serve in the arts and humanities. Others, more competent in researching the hard sciences while living abroad, will subsequently need to add more discipline-specific suggestions. With this caveat in mind, however, those researching in the hard sciences may find some of these tips and tools either directly or indirectly beneficial for their own research.

One final note: some of these tips and tools, especially those related to current technology, may prove rather elementary for my tech savvy reader. At the risk of being overly simplistic, I choose to include every applicable tip and tool that comes to mind, regardless of how obvious their implementation may seem.

TIPS FOR THE TRADE

Oscar Wilde said, "The only thing to do with good advice is to pass it on." I can't promise that all of the following advice is "good" for everyone. After all, I do agree with Sophocles: "No enemy is worse than bad advice." But, I do think that the following 24 tips, when appropriated for your own circumstances, personality, resources, and calling, will help you research and write more productively at your new address.

Tip #1: Take a Dose of Reality

All the research tips in the world do not negate your new reality; you now live in a country different than your own. Many aspects of this new life are time consuming. Learning to navigate buses, banking, and shopping takes time. Figuring out the nuances of your university and department takes time. Situating your family to another setting takes time. And, to top it off, culture shock is no fable, and it does not quickly or quietly acquiesce. Culture shock's menacing tentacles occasionally disrupt your otherwise tranquil new routine—sometimes even years after moving to your new home. This psychological nuisance steals time. To retain your sanity as it relates to your research goals—especially if your genetic cards dealt you more of a personality Type A than a Type B—you must adjust for this extra time.

Particularly in your first year abroad, therefore, suffer no shame if your productivity is not what you hope for. It is simply unrealistic to think you'll research and write as efficiently on the mission field as you did prior to it. This is a hearty dose of reality worth swallowing from the outset. However, progress can be made. And these tips of the trade will hopefully set you on the right path. Thus, you must be realistic about what you can accomplish. There is a positive side, however. Although the output may be less, the quality may increase since the very result of living internationally can add new insights to your work (something I discuss below).

Another dose of reality is the financial expense of researching and writing productively while living internationally. Some of the

following tips can be expensive. A few of you—from the more lucrative fields—rake in substantial bling for teaching. Most of us don't. In fact, many of you likely receive (at least partially) the sacrificial support of faithful donors. If you want to research abroad, budget for it in advance.

Tip #2 : Slay the Dragon of Guilt

You've prepared your whole life to serve in your new culture with untold hours in classrooms, in front of computers composing research papers, fulfilling teaching assignments, and attending conferences. All augmented with herculean stamina in part-time jobs and, most likely, with a stellar spouse rooting for you at every juncture. The money invested in these endeavors might make Bill Gates raise a brow (upon further thought, probably not … but it is still expensive). And, to top it off, people and Churches back home probably funnel money into your ministry.

Cast on this backdrop, when the dust settles from your move, a voice from within may whisper, "What a waste of resources to spend X number of hours per week hunched over a desk with book in hand and computer powered on when there are so many students and colleagues to reach." On one level, I empathize with this sentiment; we do move abroad to teach and to build relationships. And, we should, indeed, invest a lot of time in them. However, a call to scholarship is a call to research. And, research requires time at a desk. Therefore, a call to university service should not devolve into guilt over time spent on research.

More importantly, there's a deeper issue related to philosophically polarizing research and ministry, as if they are at odds with one another. Simply put, phrasing it in such a polarizing way is a false dichotomy. Research is ministering to people—it is just delayed ministering to people. Let me explain. When I teach in the classroom or meet with students, I influence lives instantaneously. I speak words, and at that moment people change, whether slightly or significantly. Research, on the other hand, ministers to, and changes, people in the distant future, when the quality of your teaching gradually increases or when the research is finally pub-

5

lished and read by students and colleagues.   Furthermore, good research opens doors. It fosters respect in the academy, thus providing platforms that you otherwise might not have, including opportunities to give more lectures, teach certain classes, and to more easily relocate when the time arises. It also fosters respect with your peers, opening doors to share your faith because they likely value research themselves. In short, good scholarship for a professor represents a good testimony both to other scholars and to your institution. Equally important, Paul tells us, "Whatever you do, work at it with all your heart, as working for the Lord" (Colossians 3:23).

It's one thing for you, personally, to understand that research and ministry are two sides of the same philosophical coin, but it is another thing altogether for some donors back home to accept it. Perhaps you have donors who view ministry as something like this: "If it ain't preaching, it ain't ministry." I understand the sentiment. There is no getting around the fact that New Testament Christianity is directly linked with verbally sharing the Gospel. Scripture expects obedient Christians—scholars included—to actively engage unbelievers. But, do keep in mind that Paul, a man who thought Jesus could return at any moment (1 Thessalonians 4:15–18) and a man whose missional fervor led him voluntarily to an early grave (Acts 21:13), took the time to research and to write theological masterpieces (e.g., Romans). Research, then, is ministry well worth pursuing. Waste no time, therefore, in slaying the dragon of guilt when he illogically proposes to dichotomize research and ministry.

Donors can grow in their own understanding of ministry through well-rounded updates of your work. Alongside your tales from afar about culture, evangelism, family, and new friends, occasionally keep them abreast of your research and the impact it has. When appropriate, communicate to them that the Bible supports a life of the mind (e.g., the very nature of Paul's writings assumes scholarly reflection as defined by ancient standards [see also Matthew 22:37]), and relate to them that they benefit from research more than they might realize. For example, almost every fact in a

reputable Study Bible or commentary cost someone years (and, in many cases, decades) of research. As donors gradually learn these important lessons, then your guilt about spending your time researching will diminish. More importantly, your donors will grow to respect and value such an exceptionally influential ministry.

TIP #3: TAME THE TICKING CLOCK: NEGOTIATE IN ADVANCE

Clocks tick at the same pace whether you live in New York or Nepal. However, there are often more things—and certainly more unexpected things—to fit into every hour while living internationally, where routine errands like buying groceries can take twice as long. Resources abound in the West with advice on how researchers should manage the ticking clock: be disciplined, avoid procrastination, write regularly, schedule your writing, know your rhythm (are you a morning or evening writer?), take care of yourself physically (exercise, eat properly, take breaks, get enough sleep), just get started even if what you are writing is not yet good enough, eliminate distractions, secure deadlines because they can be motivating, and, finally, read good books about writing such as those by Paul Sylvia, *How to Write A Lot: A Practical Guide to Academic Writing* (American Psychological Association, 2007) and Howard S. Becker, *Writing for Social Scientists: How to Start and Finish Your Thesis, Book, or Article* (University of Chicago Press, 2007). I do not replicate their good advice here but only mention tips specifically pertinent to living overseas. Since taming the clock often proves most challenging, I give substantial space to it in the next seven tips.

Taming the clock can begin before you ever arrive on campus. In many international universities, faculty and staff are insanely overworked, and the amount of bureaucratic red tape is simply astounding. Deans and presidents frequently call last-minute meetings, and they fully expect their professors to be there, even if they had other plans for weeks in advance. You may arrive in a setting where superiors assume for you similar expectations. You can begin navigating this, if possible and if appropriate, by negotiating in advance for research time.

Understanding such negotiations relative to your new culture is imperative. Contracts and negotiations can mean something different for you than they do for your new colleagues. You might arrive on campus thinking that you and your superiors are on the same page because of what appears to you as a clearly written contract, when actually you might not even be in the same book! Because cultures are so diverse, I am unable to offer specific tips on navigating these interchanges. A good resource to begin with is Scott Moreau's, Evvy Campbell's, and Susan Greener's new book, *Effective Intercultural Communication: A Christian Perspective* (Baker Academic, 2014). My general advice here is, after arriving at your new post, to gently remind your superiors in culturally sensitive ways of your agreements about research. Ask your new, national colleagues how to do this effectively and sensitively, and remember that this may require a delicate touch. On the one hand, you need time to research. On the other hand, you don't want to inadvertently play the role of the dictatorial foreigner demanding his or her hegemonic ways.

Negotiating for this time will mutually benefit both you and the institution. For you, obviously, it affords time to pursue an important part of your academic calling. For the institution, it reinforces the fact that time spent on research can benefit their own university. It enhances pedagogy and increases professor morale. Furthermore, it encourages university personnel to think long term. For example, it might challenge them to incrementally come to understand that the financial benefits of each professor teaching twelve classes per semester are short-lived because, over the long haul, quality decreases.

TIP #4: TAME THE TICKING CLOCK:
   DON'T REINVENT THE WHEEL

With a reality check in place, unnecessary guilt addressed, and negotiations sought in advance, undergird all the advice that follows with this tip: ask your new local colleagues how they go about their research and how they navigate the administrative structures of their institution. It would, after all, be presumptuous at worst

and a comical oversight at best to ask how to research abroad and never explore answers with nationals who have already done it for years. Find out from them how your new institution regards research, rewards it, encourages it, and interprets it.

TIP #5: TAME THE TICKING CLOCK:
    FIND THE RIGHT PLACE AND TIME

With your superiors (hopefully) on board and with advice in hand from your new colleagues, finding an actual place to research can prove especially challenging, even if your institution provides an office. Your office may be noisy, crowded, prone to interruptions, filled with cigarette smoke, and perhaps has no access to clean restrooms! Part of your negotiations may include time away from the office for research. Your new house or apartment may be the best location. However, your new residence may be too small, especially if you have a family. As with many aspects of your new life, you will need to be creative. Maybe there is a quiet and remote place in the library, a vacant room somewhere on campus, or a restaurant or coffee shop down the street. If affordable in your city, routine stays at a local hotel could offer you the tranquility needed to push your work forward. If forced to research in a loud office or at a small desk relegated to the corner of a heavily-traveled bedroom, then consider investing in noise canceling headphones. Or, simply drown out excessive noise through your cellphone earbuds (discussed further below).

Closely related to finding the right place is finding the right time to research. Different cultures have different routines. In some locales, you can easily research in the evenings after supper. In other locales, you might need to wake up early to make it work. Many Nigerian scholars, so I am told, take a weekend or a week off at a retreat center, away from phone, family, work, and other interruptions, to write intensively.

TIP #6: TAME THE TICKING CLOCK: BACK UP YOUR DATA

In many cultural contexts, viruses, thieving, and electricity-fried electronics are much more frequent than back home. I suggest some tools in the next section for backing up your data. Here, I need only to mention that you should have a plan in place for lost information.

TIP #7: TAME THE TICKING CLOCK: RECRUIT HELP FROM LOCALS

Most of these first several tips about taming the ticking clock cost little more than your time and ingenuity. The next two tips cost money, but they may be worth it, depending on your particular situation and budget. You might consider employing help from two types of locals. First, hire one or more student assistants. Back home, universities and seminaries frequently provide graders. Usually, this is not the case abroad. But, you can hire your own graders, and even expand their responsibilities to include running errands, showing you quicker ways to do things, and helping you navigate language barriers. Additionally, if you have a particularly competent student or two, then you can hire them to help you research and write. Most students will excitedly jump at the opportunity to work with you a few hours a week. Beyond freeing up some of your time, this also allows you to invest more deeply in one or two students, and, to their benefit, it adds experience to their developing résumé and helps them pay for their tuition and their travels to and from school. For those that more specifically help you research and write, you will especially invest in the next generation of scholars.

Second, employ a house cleaner. Investing in someone to clean is, at least for me, internally conflicting, as it can smack of elitism. After all, as so many people (perhaps justifiably) assume, only the über-wealthy pay others to clean for them. This is precisely, for good reason, what you do not want your donors to think. For this reason, among others, my wife and I have not hired a house cleaner in China. If we had three toddlers traipsing around Shanghai with us, then we might reconsider! The fact is, however, that there are usually significant differences between hiring a cleaner in your

new locale and in hiring one back home. For one, house cleaners back home are generally quite expensive while, in most places abroad, they are very affordable. Additionally, the time it takes to accomplish routine things in your new culture, especially with kids, increases significantly. Hiring a house cleaner in most countries is not only an affordable time-saver, but it often provides a good job for a needy person. Equally important, this person frequently grows close to your family, thus providing ministry opportunities otherwise not afforded.

TIP #8: TAME THE TICKING CLOCK: TRAVEL WISELY

Another potentially expensive tip that helps save time is to use "research friendly" means of travel. If you live where frequent travel is necessary, then strategically choosing how you travel will give you hours of extra time to accomplish certain tasks. Take Shanghai, for example. You can travel locally by foot, bicycle, electric bicycle, bus, subway, or taxi. Faster and more convenient means of travel, such as taxis, cost more money. Although taxis are an expensive mode of travel, it provides the best setting to read, check emails, return texts, and plan meetings. Thus, at times it may be wiser to spend an hour sitting in a taxi with laptop open than standing in a crowded subway.

TIP #9: TAMING THE TICKING CLOCK: RELEARN "YES" AND "NO"

You have likely learned appropriate ways in your native language to politely say "yes" or "no" to a colleague's invitation or suggestion. You may need to relearn this skill at your new university because saying "yes" and "no" is not as simple in some cultures as simply saying "yes" and "no"! My monocultural friends may balk at this, because it seems like a terribly absurd suggestion. Expats who live in Asia, however, will respond with an understanding nod. In an attempt to "save and give face," my Chinese friends and colleagues, for example, will often avoid directly saying "no," though both parties in the conversation are expected to understand clearly that "no" has been communicated.

Knowledge of this simple fact would have saved me a lot of confusion a few years ago in an email exchange with a Vietnamese professor who had invited me to present a paper at a conference in Ho Chi Minh City. He politely asked me to change the title of my paper, "Science Emerging in China with Religion-Like Characteristics." He wanted me to replace the word "China" with "Asia." The professor did not tell me something that I learned much later from another source, that he was trying to avoid losing face with his colleagues because of my specific—possibly negative—mention of China. Relative to my American, academic culture, I humbly challenged his suggestion that I change my title, and, though honestly open to changing it, I provided solid reasons to keep "China" in my title. The most important reason for me to retain "China" was that my knowledge of the rest of Asia was simply too limited.

Instead of my rhetoric communicating to him, "I am open to what you're saying, but let's discuss this more," it, instead, communicated, "No! I am not going to change the title of my paper." I failed to know this! As a result, he told me: "No, you cannot present that paper at our conference." But, the way he communicated this "no" was lost on me at the time: he invited me to present the paper at a conference later that year, when, he explained, it would be better received. To me, he was not saying "no," but "wait." So, I was thrilled to get to travel, albeit later, to Vietnam to present my paper! I learned subsequently, however, that there was really no conference later that year! In his mind, he was not ambiguous; he clearly communicated "no." Case closed. Why did he communicate "no" in such an indirect way? He did not want me, a fellow professor, to lose face because of rejection. He was actually being polite. But, I thought he really wanted me to present my paper at another time. Knowing this would have prevented the string of embarrassingly awkward emails that followed!

The world's cultures are too diverse and too complex for me to offer specific advice about how to say "yes" and "no" in every context. My tip here is simple: through whatever means—conversations with expats and locals, reading books about the culture, and/or inquiring from Google—learn how to say "yes" and "no" and

12

then apply it appropriately with your colleagues to free up more time for research.

Tip #10: Tame the Ticking Clock: A Caveat and Some Perspective

Before wrapping things up about taming the ticking clock, allow me to make an important caveat and provide some perspective. First, a caveat. Managing time to allow for research abroad requires a delicate balance. Part of the reason for serving internationally is to practice missional hospitality to students and colleagues (Christopher J. Freet, *A New Look at Hospitality as a Key to Missions*, Energion Publications, 2014) and to immerse yourself in a new culture, while refusing to hermit away in an office every day. You don't want to withdraw from the very culture that you're there to learn and serve.

Striking this balance depends a lot on your own personality. My more extroverted colleagues frequently leave their office doors open and beckon students to drop in unexpectedly and never seem to experience decreasing academic output because of it. In fact, they draw energy from it. My more introverted colleagues, conversely, still love to meet with students but usually need advanced notice in order to psychologically prepare for the encounter so as not to deplete their emotional resources. If America is your home culture and if you find yourself leaning more toward the introversion side of the continuum, then perhaps you have felt pressure to feel guilty about your regulated isolation. Don't fall prey, however, to the arbitrarily imposed assumption that extroversion is some type of objective ideal (see Susan Cain, *Quiet: The Power of Introverts in a World that Can't Stop Talking*, Broadway Books, 2013). Most of the world's population, namely in Asia, are more introverted than extroverted. Jesus, too, often sought isolation (John 6:15).

Also, a word about perspective, especially for my more "Type A" colleagues. I have been discussing how to "Tame the Ticking Clock." This phrase has Western sentiments dripping from every corner. Keep in mind that you might serve in a culture where "the clock" does not mean the same as it does for you. For many, the

clock ranks dozens of rungs down the ladder of importance, behind things like "saving face" or "talking about the weather." Adjusting to a different set of expectations about time, especially for Type A personalities, can be a beautiful exercise in spiritual formation. Perhaps a healthy perspective is to follow the advice I received from a friend who teaches in an undisclosed location in Africa: "Ideally, you want to conform your standards and routines as much as possible to those of your national colleagues. Find out what everyone else does when the lights go out. If they just sit and chat with neighbors, then maybe you should do the same thing too!"

With this caveat, this perspective, and these time saving tips in place, when your scheduled research time arrives—*and this is important*—use that time for research!

TIP #11: ORDER AN EXTRA DOSE OF PATIENCE

Although you do everything possible to tame the clock, it will still be more frustratingly challenging at times than back in your home country. If you move to China, for example, it will likely take weeks to iron out the wrinkles of navigating internet censorship (see discussion below about VPNs). Or, if you move to Nigeria, adjusting to intermittent electricity and employee strikes will cause frustration. There will likely come a time, after the internet fails or the electricity goes out, when you drop your head and, with blood pressure rising, threaten to give up all hope of any productive research. Don't throw your computer through the window! Be patient with yourself (Galatians 5:22). Be patient with your new environment. In time, you will find more productive means to accomplish your research.

TIP #12: TAP INTO A WELL OF ENCOURAGEMENT AND MOTIVATION

As your patience decreases, your encouragement and motivation may decline with it. As time consuming endeavors that are so simple to accomplish back home continue to crowd out research, a longing to toss in the towel may become appealing. Adding insult to injury, your university or department may not value research as

much as you do. Or, worse, they may never even think about it. Although with time and discipline you might acquire the patience of Job, you may still on occasion become discouraged and unmotivated. When this happens, remember your calling. If you are called to research, then God will provide the time to do it. Ask for help from your spouse and family to hold you accountable to stick to it. Or, find a research accountability partner either back home or in your new culture. And, be encouraged knowing that, as leading missiologist Timothy Tennent once quipped, the Apostle Paul was simultaneously one of the world's greatest missionaries and at the same time one of the world's greatest theologians. Few researchers have contributed more than Paul to the advancement of a particular field. Be encouraged! You can concomitantly research and be a missionary.

TIP #13: PLAN AHEAD FOR UNEXPECTED DOWN TIME

Regardless of how much you plan ahead and no matter how patient you are, inevitably life abroad will deal you a healthy dose of unwanted downtime. Right in the middle of writing an article, the electricity will go out or the internet will crash; en route to your favorite café for some scheduled writing, a traffic jam will leave you for two hours in the backseat of a cab; or, a student protest will provide you an unexpected holiday. Appropriating some of the right tools that I discuss in the next section will keep you researching during such interruptions. At this point, suffice it to say: be prepared for it! For example, if electricity is unreliable, then always have hard copies of materials on hand so that you can continue working. If you travel on unpredictable roads, even for short trips to the grocery store, or if you live in a culture where meetings rarely begin on time, then always carry along work materials. Be prepared in advance to work offline in the following ways: compose outgoing emails in your favorite word processor and save them to send later (or use Gmail Offline or a similar platform that I discuss in the next section); cut and paste important emails into a word processor for convenient viewing; and transfer articles, blogs, and websites to some of the apps discussed below.

There is another challenge particularly relevant for the academic missionary that often leads to unwanted downtime. Somewhere amidst the smooth sailing of your research, you will come across a much needed book or article that is snugly nestled in a library somewhere on the other side of Planet Earth. Back home, remedying this problem was easy; simply walk across the courtyard to the library and check it out, make copies, or order it through inter-library loan. When in The Gambia, however, this can bring your research to a grinding halt because only someone from home can get it for you. The next four tips offer some practical advice on navigating this specific challenge. Here, I simply suggest to be prepared for it. One way to prepare is to work on several projects at once, including the writing of popular pieces that require fewer resources (like the book you are currently reading!). When a hard-to-get resource is frustratingly out of reach, then set into motion the process of retrieving it by using the next several tips and, while you wait, move on to another project.

Tip #14: Hire an Assistant from Your Home Country

I can hardly overstate the help provided by an assistant from home. This is likely one of the most important tips I offer, and every researcher living abroad should consider it. Here are three things to know about hiring an assitant from home. First, you need to decide who to hire. The best assistants from home are undergraduate or (preferably) graduate students who live on or near a campus with a library that fits your needs. These students often look for part time, flexible work with low demands to augment their other employment. Related to this, consider hiring two assistants (one that you promise a certain number of hours weekly and another one who works as needed) so that if one quits unexpectedly or is unable to perform a certain task, then your research can continue unhindered.

Second, decide what types of things that they can do for you. They can scan and email you articles and portions of books that cannot be accessed abroad. Especially helpful is that most university and seminary libraries today provide free scanning. They can edit

16

your newsletters and build bibliographies for you. Depending on their ability, they can even edit and write for you. The number of hours per week or month can be as flexible as your needs. I have hired assistants to work on an as-needed basis, while others have worked 5 hours per month and at 10 hours per week. Finally, you will need to advertise for an assistant. The easiest way is to post an advertisement for the position on campus bulletin boards and/ or at campus websites. If you do not live near the campus, usually you can find a professor, staff member, or a colleague who will sympathize with your mission and be glad to help. Simply email them your job description and have them post it for you. An easy way to hire subsequent assistants is, once the first one moves on, to ask him or her to recommend any friends who might be interested in working for you.

Hiring an assistant benefits not only your research, but it also benefits the employee and (perhaps) your new, national colleagues in several influential ways. It often provides a mentoring relationship between you and your assistants. It gives them opportunity to work internationally, exposing them to other cultures. Also, it can increase their interest in missions. And, occasionally, if you have the money to pay them for extra hours, you might ask your assistants to help a local, national scholar obtain resources for a project.

TIP #15: UTILIZE VOLUNTEERS FROM YOUR HOME COUNTRY

A few strategic volunteers can complement your paid assistants. In most circumstances, volunteers cannot replace paid assistants because paid assistants live on, or next to a campus, and their job is to react quickly to your requests. But, volunteers can save you money, for example, by ordering a needed book and mailing it to you, by running errands, or by making a few needed phone calls. If you are blessed to have volunteers who live near a library, then they can take on some of your assistants' responsibilities, further saving you money.

Tip #16: Get to Know a Librarian

An ideal volunteer is a librarian (or a library employee) who sympathizes with your calling. He or she can help you obtain sources that few others can. He or she need not work at a world class library, although that would be best. Remember, modern inter-library loan systems are fabulous. So, a community college librarian may prove more helpful than first meets the eye.

Tip #17: Email an Author

Occasionally, you might need an article that you or your assistant simply can't find. Or, you may be faced with buying an expensive monograph, just for a chapter or two from it. In such cases, consider contacting the author directly to ask for a PDF of the article or a specific section of the monograph. Often, if you explain your situation, including the sacrifices you're making to serve internationally where national scholars are not afforded the luxury to do what Western scholars so freely and easily do, they are often eager, and honored, to help.

The same applies for conference papers. Often the expense and time involved in traveling to conferences are too high for you to attend. However, if you see advertised a presentation that might benefit your research, a brief perusal of the internet often turns up an email address for the presenter. In my experience, presenters are usually flattered that I am interested in their work and are eager to help scholars in our situation by passing along their papers and notes.

Your situation may differ, but I have never had a professor turn me down after I explain my situation. On one occasion, I needed a German book that my assistant and I simply could not find. I contacted the author in Germany, and he kindly and quickly mailed me a copy by snail mail, all the way to China!

Tip #18: Collaborate with Colleagues Back Home

Collaborating with peers is wise regardless of where you live. It provides accountability, better perspective, and it cuts the workload in half. Collaborating with scholars back home has some added benefits. They can, for example, help you obtain resources and keep you abreast of quickly changing academic fields. Furthermore, your new life abroad, as mentioned above and as discussed more fully below, will likely benefit your research projects because of the fresh perspectives your international experience brings to the table.

Tip #19: Collaborate with Colleagues in your New Culture

Collaboration with colleagues in your new culture can also ease some of the burdens of researching abroad. The benefits are generally the same as collaborating with colleagues back home, but with some added challenges and benefits. Challenges include the following. First, differing perspectives on time and deadlines may cause misunderstandings. Second, if you plan to publish your results in English and if English is your colleague's second language, then you will likely bear extra editing responsibilities. Conversely, if you plan to publish your results in your new host language and if you are not conversant in it, then you will ultimately have to trust your colleague's translation. Finally, there are often unstated but assumed differences of social power that can lead to miscommunication and misunderstandings; in other words, your colleague may see you as "more powerful" simply because you are a foreigner, and thus communicate with you differently (e.g., afraid to say "no" directly) (see Moreau, et al, *Effective Intercultural Communication*, chapter 12). On most occasions, you can overcome these challenges by assuming a proper posture of humility—by "considering [your national colleague] as better than yourself" (Philippians 2:3).

The benefits of collaborating with your new colleagues, however, probably outweigh the challenges. Working with a colleague who understands the local academy can help with a host of things. They are better connected in your new country than you are, more intricately understand local needs, can better research locally, and

can translate work into local languages if needed. Aside from helping you do better research, collaborating with a national colleague will help you be a better researcher. As a missionary, you well know the benefits of working with people from other countries (e.g., exposure to new perspectives on life); research is no different.

Finally, beyond benefiting you and your research, collaborating with a colleague can benefit them for all of the same reasons it benefits you. But, there may be extra benefits for them. In low-income countries, resources are often hard to find; by collaborating with you, nationals will have access to resources that they otherwise could never use. Closely related to this, collaborating with nationals, especially those who cannot access good resources, will help develop their research skills.

TIP #20: BE CAREFUL WITH INFORMED CONSENT

If your research requires interviews with locals, then know that informed consent procedures can be tricky, because nationals may not understand exactly what it means. Given the dangers often involved for people in many countries, it is always best to err on the side of caution when using real names. For example, careless journalists recently published the names of Boko Haram victims in Nigeria, which placed them in grave danger. If you doubt whether your interviewee understands the informed consent process, then strongly consider using a pseudonym.

TIP #21: CONSCIOUSLY FOLLOW ETHICAL GUIDELINES

In some settings, research methods might be unethical, but they are practiced for the sake of convenience. Examples might include plagiarism, ill treatment of others, bribery, and fees for publishing. As Christ's representatives, we need to set the pace for what is ethically appropriate with our research, resisting the urge to take short cuts at the expense of our integrity and at the expense of others. The challenge, of course, is that navigating ethical conundrums in your new culture will not always be black-and-white. Take, for instance, publication fees for journals which are usually

scorned in the West but are mandatory in Nigeria where there are no rich publishing companies to subsidize the efforts. It is beyond the scope of this book—and well beyond my expertise—to offer an ethical rubric for your research abroad. My best advice is to learn the particular nuances of your new host culture, be immersed in Scripture, have at least a working knowledge of the discipline of ethics in general and of ethics relative to your new context, and, finally, expect on occasion to have your sense of morality challenged.

Tip #22: Learn to Love E-Reading

A decade or so ago pundits often debated the future of e-books. "Will e-books displace traditional hardbacks," they pondered? "Will libraries go the way of dinosaurs? Will e-books be around in 50 years?" Although I cannot predict the place of hardbacks and libraries in the lives of tomorrow's bibliophiles, I confidently predict that e-reading is here to stay. Amazon's ultimate goal, for example, is to make its entire 1.8 million volume library accessible in e-book format. All readers, but especially academic missionaries, will benefit from transitioning, at least in part, to electronic devices. My colleague who serves in an undisclosed location in Africa offered this quip in a personal correspondence about researching abroad: "You can't even get off the ground without [an e-reader]!" I evaluate in my next section the current electronic devices on the market. Here, I simply mention the benefits of learning to love e-reading.

Some of my readers in their 20s and early 30s, with a scratch of the head, may wonder who in the modern west does not read materials in e-format? But people from my generation (the middle-aged crowd) sometimes struggle to adjust to reading and researching on a digital device. The feel of a book in their hand is simply too natural, easy, and irresistible. "Flipping through the pages" of an e-book is awkward and cumbersome. I resonate! At 40 years old, I never read my first e-book until my mid-thirties. Five years later, believe it or not, I prefer e-books to hardbacks. My notes and highlights are searchable, buying books on the go via the web is simple, traveling with a hundred pdf files is no problem, navigating my book is easy, switching between books is a breeze, looking up words in

a dictionary is a tap away, enlarging font for ailing eyes takes only one click, and I can quit reading on page 78 on my iPad and pick up my iPhone and continue reading on page 78!

I must admit, the transition is difficult, but it is doable. Throughout my undergrad, graduate, and PhD studies, I never once read an e-book. The mission field forced me to use them. And, I am glad it did. The academic payoff is worth it, not to mention the freedom it provides while traveling is priceless. So, bite the bullet, begin building your electronic library, dive into an e-book or two, and learn to love them.

Tip #23: You Still Need Hardback Books

Although you now adore e-books more than ever, you will still need the occasional hardback because many books—especially academic ones—are not yet available in e-format and because in most cases you cannot share or loan e-books to colleagues. You can get needed hardback books by planning ahead in several ways. First, simply bring them with you on your flights. Since weight dictates price when checking bags on all airlines, bring books in your carry-on luggage. Second, if colleagues, friends, or friends of friends are traveling through, then ask them to bring books for you. Third, have someone mail them to you. Be careful with this last suggestion, however. Not only is it expensive, but given the varying quality of postal services around the world, your books may never arrive. Finally, if all else fails and if copyright laws permit, have your assistant or volunteer scan the entire book and email it to you. If copyright laws do not permit scanning books, then contact the publisher, explain your situation, ask them for a PDF copy of the book, and offer to pay for it.

Tip #24: Where to Publish

After you have slain the dragon of guilt, tamed the ticking clock, increased your patience, navigated downtime, hired assistants, rounded up some volunteers back home, strategized with

colleagues, taken care with informed consent, learned to love e-reading, and, with a large helping of God's wonderful grace, proven to yourself that you can research and write abroad, it is now time to submit your work for publication. But where?

If possible—that is, if there are publishing venues available—you should try to advance scholarship in your new host country by writing papers, articles, textbooks, monographs, etc. Or, at least you will likely want to find creative ways to disseminate scholarship from abroad in your new setting. If publishing venues are not available, then you may want to initiate one or two such venues in cooperation with competent national scholars. When publishing locally, you need to consult more intentionally with national colleagues because you may need to avoid many subtle, unspoken expectations (like unstated submission guidelines or politically sensitive words).

You probably already aspire to these kinds of goals because they reside so deeply at the heart of what we do as academic missionaries. But, should you spend your limited time trying to publish in what are generally flooded markets back home, thus taking time away from your service abroad? The answer probably depends on your discipline. Perhaps your field is internationalized enough to make the point moot; that is, it is irrelevant where you publish your research because all of your new, international colleagues and students will read it anyway. However, the case may differ if, for example, your field is theology because a theologian in Africa has the option to publish in several reputable African Journals that largely (and unfortunately) go unread and uncited in the West.

If you do have a choice where to publish, then how exactly do you choose? Ultimately, only you can prayerfully adjudicate that decision based on your gifts, opportunities, goals, and interests. With that said, perhaps a both/and, rather than an either/or, approach is better. Publishing in your new culture is advantageous for what I trust are obvious reasons. Back home, it is quite likely that colleagues need scholarship from those who have lived at length in other cultures and, as a result, have gained new insights into their respective disciplines. A specific example of cross-cultural experi-

ence that advanced a particular discipline that I mention in my article, "The American Evangelical Academy and the World," is the work of Timothy Laniak, Professor of Old Testament and Academic Dean at Gordon-Conwell Theological Seminary in Charlotte, N.C:

> [Laniak says that] living with Bedouin in Israel and Egypt helped inform his biblical theology of leadership, *Shepherds After My Own Heart: Pastoral Traditions and Leadership in the Bible* [Downers Grove: InterVarsity, 2006, p.13]. [He] elsewhere confirms how serving at length internationally gave him insights into Scripture that he otherwise would never have had: "Listening to Christian leaders in other parts of the world constantly challenged my interpretation of Scripture" ["My Journey: A Personal Word from Tim Laniak" <http://shepherd-leader.com/about.php>, accessed April 12, 2015].

Aside from the mutual benefits that your previous and new culture will gain from this both/and approach, it will, hopefully, help ameliorate the unhealthy tendency toward western academic hegemony.

TOOLS FOR THE TRADE

All researchers need tools for the work they do—books, computers, journals, etc. While living abroad you need these tools and more. Specifically, you need ones best suited for international life where travel-difficulties, power outages, and daily nuisances are the norm. Mentioning every tool available to any given researcher is impossible and unnecessary. Here I only mention tools most helpful for academic missionaries. I should emphasize again what I have highlighted numerous times above: none of these tools provide the convenience of a cozy, predictable, office back home. But using the following tools, the ones that fit your particular budget and situation, can make your research abroad go as smoothly as possible.

TOOL #1: ELECTRONIC DEVICES: THE iPAD

The iPad. Expensive? Yes. Quite helpful? Without a doubt. Why so helpful? Because it provides a research platform beyond your computer that, in my experience, no other digital device provides. The iPad has its drawbacks: extensive typing is cumbersome (unless you purchase a keyboard; see below), there are no backspace or tab keys, and, as just mentioned, it is pricey. The pros, however, far outweigh the cons. Think of the iPad as a multifunctional tool comparable to a Swiss Army Knife. First, it gives you more mobility with your research than does a computer. It is much easier and quicker, for example, to use an iPad instead of a laptop on a crowded bus or in a taxi; I am, for example, typing these words on a cramped, Shanghai bus. Second, the iPad will keep your research going when your electricity goes out, or if your computer crashes or is stolen. Finally, it is the best e-reader on the market with every major bookseller represented in Apple's app market, thus allowing you to travel with an extensive library.

I suggest investing in the standard size iPad instead of the iPad Mini because the screen on the standard size gives you the feel of reading a normal-sized book instead of reading only partial pages. This proves especially helpful when reading PDFs. Additionally, I suggest investing in a good iPad case since you will likely travel in

rugged places. I certainly do not recommend Apple's iPad case. It is too flimsy, cheaply made, and it does not sturdily hold the iPad upright.

Tool #2: Electronic Devices: Other Tablets

To save money, you may be tempted to rely solely on a Kindle Fire or some other similarly affordable tablet. With all things equal, a cheaper tablet may serve your needs fine. But, all things are not equal. You need the best tablet for research while living abroad. The size and functionality of the iPad make it the best option for this. Falling for the temptation to save money on cheaper tablets will result in only frustration and hindered research.

Now that I have sufficiently hailed the iPad as a superb tool for researching in your new host country, and in an attempt to avoid propagating an unnecessary tech-elitism, let me say a few words about other tablets. E-ink e-readers may serve as a nice supplement for the iPad, especially for users who live in countries that experience extended power outages. In layman's terms, an e-ink e-reader is a digital device that lets you store and read books, the pages of which resemble traditionally printed pages (with black-and-white type) instead of a computer screen. Excluded from these devices are the bells and whistles of beautifully-displayed colored pages, apps, and music. Although you can connect to Wi-Fi with these devices, web-surfing is practically impossible because their wireless connectivity is primarily designed for purchasing books.

However, the benefits of e-ink e-readers are twofold. First, and most importantly, these devices frequently have nearly a one month battery life! Contrast with the iPad that will only last a full day with light usage. The e-ink e-reader's long battery life proves especially helpful for those experiencing extended power outages. Secondly, these devices are a good choice for those who read outside, because the iPad is virtually useless in direct sunlight or bright light.

The best e-ink e-reader on the market for researchers is the very affordable Kindle by Amazon. There are several varieties (e.g., "Kindle Paperwhite" and "Kindle Keyboard") that basically do the same things but have different features. The Kindle is better than,

say, the Nook because of Amazon's superior selection of e-books. Aside from purchasing and reading books, the Kindle lets you download and read PDFs, syncs nicely with the iPad, and many have 3G capabilities. Do not confuse Kindle e-ink e-readers with the Kindle Fire, another product from Amazon. The Kindle Fire is similar in appearance and function to an iPad, the size of which is between the regular iPad and the iPad Mini. If you own an iPad, the Kindle Fire is unnecessary because the iPad will do everything the Kindle Fire can do and much, much more.

TOOL #3: ELECTRONIC DEVICES: iPHONE

Like the Kindle, the iPhone supplements the iPad. I specifically recommend the iPhone over other phones because, if you accept my advice about the iPad and Kindle, then the iPhone is your most logical choice in cell phones because it syncs so smoothly with the other devices. The iPhone's size and accessibility are precisely its advantage for quick reading, studying, and reviewing in crowded busses, subways, and supermarkets. Whereas you have to dig into a backpack or briefcase to retrieve an iPad or Kindle, the iPhone snaps easily onto your belt, drops in a purse, or slides into a back pocket.

The best use of the iPhone, because of its size, is not so much for reading articles or books while traveling around town, though you can use it in that way within limits. Rather, it is best used to study and review things that can more easily be done while riding in a cab for 20 minutes. What kinds of things do I have in mind? Most likely you will have to study a new language (or stay fresh with research languages) when you move abroad. Myriads of language acquisition apps are available that provide the perfect platform for brief intermittent study while skipping through town, thus eliminating antiquated and cumbersome flashcards. Or, to offer other examples, with the iPhone you can review class notes, meeting agendas, and brainstorm ideas while in quick transit. The 20 minutes used during these brief forays of study or review equates to 20 minutes of office time that you can reallocate for more detailed research.

Tool #4: Computer with no Handheld Devices

My love for handheld devices and my biased bent toward their utility for research surfaces clearly in the previous three tools (iPad, other tablets, and iPhone), and you may get the impression that it is impossible to research abroad without them or without the current apps that they offer (discussed below). Now permit me to make a qualification: you are not doomed to an academically unproductive stay in your host culture without these tools. In many cases, they simply streamline your research, especially if you travel. They make reading e-documents and e-books easier than a computer, and they provide alternatives for remaining productive during power outages. However, my colleague who teaches in an undisclosed location in Southeast Asia related to me, "I have none of these [devices], yet...I have become more productive in [my new country of service] than I ever was in the United States. So [research] is still possible for those of us in laptop land." Hopefully this is good news if you are on a restricted budget.

If you do stay in laptop land, then few things electronically will likely change about how you conduct your research, though you may want to consider some of the programs mentioned next.

Tool #5: Apps and Computer Programs

Owning the right devices is one thing. Maximizing their use for research while abroad is another thing. The market is saturated with apps; and computer programs will specifically help maximize your research efforts, either by directly making researching abroad easier or by indirectly freeing up more time to use for research. Mentioning every available app and program is, of course, impossible. Rather, I can only mention here a representative sampling. Although I mention most apps and programs by company name, remember that, nearly always, competitors who offer similar products might better meet your specific needs. So, I encourage you to see my suggestions more as a general guide than as a prescribed trek. I only discuss here apps and programs that will generally appeal to researchers more broadly and do not discuss field-specific apps or

programs (e.g., Logos Bible for Bible researchers). Finally, I do not discuss websites (such as the wonderfully helpful Google Books) because there are simply too many to address, and I assume you already know what sites are most apropos for your specific discipline.

A = App only
AC = App and Computer program

The Amazon app and website is primarily intended to help you shop at amazon.com, but it is also useful for research. Many of their books are searchable, and most include a table of contents.

Calibre (AC) is a free e-book library management program that offers the following features: library management, e-book conversion, syncing of all e-book reader devices, conversion of pdf's into e-book formats, and downloading news from the web and converting it into e-book form.

Clear (A) is an exceptionally intuitive, elegant, and free to-do list that syncs across all Mac products.

Docusign Ink (A) lets you sign documents from abroad.

Dropbox (AC) works as a folder on your desktop that stores your documents online so that you can access them from other devices while on the go. It is ideal for sharing and editing documents with others and for backing up your data.

EndNote and *Zotero* (C) are reference management software packages used to manage bibliographies and references when writing articles, essays, dissertations, books, and monographs.

Evernote (AC) is a wonderful platform to make notes (including audio and video), compile research, brainstorm, edit pdf's, and collect web articles. These documents are then accessible across all devices and can be shared with others. A downside to the free version of Evernote is that you must be online to use it.

Gmail Offline (AC) is a Google Chrome app that lets you read and manage messages when you don't have an internet connection and then automatically sends the messages when you reconnect to the internet. Compare with similar features available with Mozilla Thunderbird and Microsoft Outlook.

Googledocs (AC) is a word processor that functions much like Microsoft Word except it is entirely cloud based, allowing instant, remote backup. Similar to Dropbox it allows you to share and edit documents with others, and it has optional password protection.

iBooks (AC) is Apple's e-book app that is similar to the Kindle App and comes already installed on your Apple devices, but its book-selection is smaller than that found at amazon.com.

Kindle App (AC), already alluded to above, syncs all your reading material across devices and turns your iPad or iPhone into an elegant e-reader for books, textbooks, PDFs, newspapers, magazines, and more. It also provides, at your fingertips, the vast resources available for purchase at amazon.com.

Myriads of language apps (both for your target language and for research languages) will keep you studying while on-the-go.

LogMeIn (AC) is a handy app that syncs your iPad to your laptop or home computer so that you can access your computer from your iPad. In other words, you can leave your computer at home, and, when logged into LogMeIn, your computer screen will appear on your iPad, allowing you access to folders, documents, and everything else on your computer. Its primary weakness is that both your iPad and computer must be online, making it impractical for some users while traveling. Originally, LogMeIn offered this app for free. Now it costs about $70.

Microsoft Office (AC) now offers their line of products in Apple's App Store, albeit with an expensive yearly price tag of about $100. This permits better interfacing between the iPad and PC products, including Word, Excel, and PowerPoint.

Mozy (AC) is an online, data backup service for both Windows and Mac users. It backs up your data automatically in your computer's background so that if an electrical surge fries your motherboard, then you can easily access all of your documents, pictures, and movies from another computer or device. Since Mozy runs in the background, you don't have to remember to back up your computer. In the event your computer crashes, is stolen, or is otherwise inaccessible, Mozy will save you weeks of time and headaches.

Notability (A) is helpful for those who like to "handwrite" notes instead of type them. It lets you easily "write" directly on your iPad screen with either your finger or a stylus (purchased separately online or available at most office supply stores). These notes are then easily edited (including the helpful function of cutting and pasting your own handwritten notes), stored, saved as PDFs, and/or emailed to yourself or others. A unique function of Notability is that it ingeniously lets you write with large handwriting that then is simultaneously transferred into a smaller text, which allows you to fit more words to a digital page.

Pages (AC) is Apple's free, and exceptionally user-friendly, word processor that functions similarly to Word in Microsoft Office. It interfaces well with Word documents (though expect a few minor glitches), pdf's, and other platforms. Documents in Pages sync across your devices, including PCs.

PDF Expert (A) is an exceptionally helpful app that lets you open and annotate pdf's, allowing you to make highlights and take notes on the pdf document itself. Compare with Adobe Acrobat.

Pocket (AC) lets you save websites for later viewing (both while online and offline), which conveniently permits you to catch up on blogs and online articles and reviews during power outages and while on airplanes, trains, and buses. Note that Evernote recently added a similar feature to its product line.

Prayer Notes (A) helps organize your prayer requests and keep track with when and how God answers them.

Rosetta Stone (AC) is a fabulous, though quite expensive, language acquisition tool. It is not the Holy Grail of language products as its advertisers tout. But, it is a wonderful tool to complement your language study. It is especially helpful for vocabulary and syntactical acquisition and retention.

SimplyNoise (A) provides background noise via earphones for those who struggle to concentrate in loud places.

Siri (factory installed on all newer iPhones and iPads) is Apple's, sometimes witty, digital personal assistant and knowledge navigator. Siri is software that allows you to talk with your device. "She" does things like respond to your questions by searching the internet for answers, by making appointments for you, or by looking up a contact. Most beneficial for the international researcher is Siri's voice-recognition software that allows you to dictate emails, notes, and word documents. Instead of typing responses to incessant emails that flood your inbox, simply speak your reply. Instead of typing a paragraph of your research, just speak it. Siri is good (actually, she is awesome!), but she is not perfect. She requires an internet connection, which may prove intermittently problematic in some settings. And, dictating technical aspects of an article will likely prove too difficult for her. Furthermore, she sometimes struggles to understand certain accents, like Bostonians who omit their "r's" or American Southerners who transform monosyllable words into multi-syllable words. In general, however, her accuracy makes composing many documents much easier than hand typing them. Thus, in spite of her weaknesses, Siri is well worth getting to know, as she can save valuable time, especially when plodding through emails and articles.

T&TMPD (AC) and *Donor Manager* (A; AC forthcoming) are among a number of free donor manager programs that help save time in organizing and communicating with donors. T&TMPD is sophisticated and contains extensive bells-and-whistles. The downside to T&TMPD is that it almost does too much and can be complicated and cumbersome to use. Donor Manager, on the other hand, is extremely user friendly, but it cannot perform

some of the sophisticated tasks that T&TMPD can do. For example, Donor Manager's search function is, at times, too simplistic.

TurboScan (A) turns your iPhone and iPad into a portable scanner. It is useful for scanning receipts for reimbursements, for capturing journal articles in a local library, or for generally reducing paper clutter.

A *VPN* (Virtual Private Network) (AC), which provides both a secure internet connection and access to blocked websites, is necessary in many countries where internet censorship is enforced. 12VPN and Strong VPN are two excellent choices (between $75 and $100 yearly). Some countries like China will occasionally temporarily block VPNs. These internet crackdowns can be painfully aggravating. In such circumstances, buying two VPNs may prove to be a wise investment. I do not suggest using free VPNs in internet-censored countries because they do not provide the customer-support that you will likely need from time-to-time.

Tool #6: Internet

Pay the highest price for fastest internet service available. Consider, as an additional service where available, adding 3G or 4G wireless to your iPhone or iPad for travel and for power outages. Remember that you can create a hotspot from your iPhone or iPad to provide wireless internet to other devices.

Tool #7: Travel Accessories

Whether flying across the ocean or buzzing around town, these few travel accessories will complement your research while on the go.

A six foot drop cord helps you connect to receptacles in restaurants, classrooms, or airports that are just beyond reach of your computer's charger.

A multiple outlet plug solves the frustrating problem of successfully finding a receptacle to charge your dead iPad only to see that two travelers beat you to it. With a multiple outlet plug in

hand, you politely interrupt them, ask if you can share the outlet, divide the electrical current via your multiple outlet plug, insert your six foot drop cord, move to your own space a few feet away, and return to writing your article.

For those who find it difficult to type at length on the iPad, perhaps a bluetooth keyboard is worth the investment. I particularly like Logitech's "Keys-to-Go" because it is small, rugged, easily packable, and has an astounding three month battery life. One potential drawback is that it does not come with an iPad stand.

External Battery Pack for charging cell phones, tablets, and other devices (except laptops and computers; see next entry). I suggest the RavPower 15,000mAh Deluxe Portable Charger with iSmart Technology (3rd Generation) (about $40), which will recharge an iPhone 5s seven times or an iPad one time.

Extended-life batteries for computers are helpful in locales where electrical outages are the norm or if you frequently travel long distances.

CONCLUSION: BE ENCOURAGED

As you step out in faith to live the life-of-the-mind in another country, be encouraged! Although you will leave a lot behind—family, friends, safety, and comfort—you do not have to leave behind your love for advancing your field. In other words, heeding God's call to academic missions does not have to halt your research. Rather, it can enhance it. With the right tips and tools, you can live out both of your vocational loves, mission and research. Although the advice offered in this book will not guarantee smooth sailing in the rough waters of academic missions, these tips and tools—along with those that you learn on your own—will add a refreshing and much needed breeze to your academic sails.

www.ingramcontent.com/pod-product-compliance
Lightning Source LLC
Chambersburg PA
CBHW021120020426

42331CB00004B/566